My Time at The Clinton White House

1995-1999

Colonel Mark D. Gelhardt, Sr.

ERICKA

TO A FELLOW GEEK

ERICKA

TO A FERVOW ...

Copyrighted Material

Cover design and website support provided by
Gelhardt Graphics and Rob Gelhardt

First Edition, Oct 2018

ISBN 978-0-9997584-1-0

$25.00
ISBN 978-0-9997584-1-0
52500>

9 780999 758410

DEDICATION

Thanks to my lovely wife, Karen,
for encouraging me to write this book.

Thanks to Matt and Sara for the road
trip that showed me I had enough
material to put into a book.

Thanks to Laura for the editing help.

But mostly – Thanks to David and Kris
for all the support while I was working
at The White House.

PROLOGUE

Nothing in this book is classified.

All material in this book has been thoroughly researched to ensure that everything talked about is currently in the public domain.

My Time at The Clinton White House 1995 – 1999

Table of Contents

- Finding the Job
- Getting the Job
- The Call
- Interview Week
- Becoming Yankee White
- Running The White House from Cairo
- The Move

- Arriving at My New Unit
- My New Job – or So I thought?
- Learning Top-Security Stuff
- The 18 Acres (The White House Grounds)
- The White House Badge
- The Bat Phone - at Home
- Learning Multiple Jobs – at the Same Time
- The Bat Phone Rings

ABOUT THE AUTHOR

Colonel Mark D. Gelhardt, Sr.

Colonel Mark Gelhardt, had an atypical Army career that landed him next to The President of the United States, where he was responsible for the last link of communications between the President and the rest of the government.

Cadet Gelhardt entered his military service in the Reserve Officer Training Corps (ROTC) program at The University of Florida. His ROTC class became the first ever to win back to back The Warrior of Pacific trophy as the best Cadet program in the nation both his Junior (1978) and Senior years (1979). As a Cadet, Mark received the opportunity to attend Airborne school with the active Army and was awarded his Airborne wings. When Cadet Gelhardt graduated from the University of Florida he was commissioned into the United States Army, Adjutant General Corps as a Second Lieutenant (2LT). After graduation 2LT Gelhardt was sent to Fort Benjamin Harrison, Indianapolis, Indiana where he went through

Adjutant General's (AG) Officer Basic Course (OBC). 2LT Gelhardt graduated in the top 10% of his class and was immediately picked up for a special Department of the Army program as one of only ten AG 2LT selected Army wide. This test program was to teach brand new AG 2LTs to be a Chief Administration Officer of a Battalion size unit. 2LT Gelhardt stayed at Fort Benjamin Harrison for several more months, going through this first ever test program training. At the conclusion of training 2LT Gelhardt was the only 2LT to be assigned to a front-line Infantry unit, the 2nd Battalion, 504th Airborne Infantry, 1st Bridge, 82nd Airborne Division, Fort Bragg (Fayetteville), North Carolina. 2LT Gelhardt was assigned as the Battalions S1 (Chief Administration Officer for a unit of about 500 soldiers). While assigned to this Airborne Battalion, 2LT Gelhardt attended Winter Warfare school in Alaska and Jungle Expert school in the Panama Canal Zone. After the 82nd 2LT Gelhardt had the opportunity to join the Command Staff for the Headquarters, Reserve Officer Training Corps (ROTC) at Fort Bragg. During this time, he was promoted to First Lieutenant (1LT). 1LT Gelhardt was in charge of all the administration for the ROTC Advance Camp that managed over 10,000 cadets and over 1000 Army Officers and Non-Commissioned Officers (NCOs). 1LT Gelhardt excelled in this position and was awarded the Outstanding Young Officer award for Fort Bragg. 1LT Gelhardt was then transferred back to Fort Benjamin Harrison to attend the Adjutant General (AG) Officer Advance Course (OAC). 1LT Gelhardt was again in the top of his class and was awarded a Regular Army Commission and at the same time was promoted to Captain (CPT). CPT Gelhardt was assigned as an active component advisor to the 87th Maneuver Area Command

(MAC) in Hoover, Alabama a suburb of Birmingham, Alabama. During this time with the 87th CPT Gelhardt attended several Army schools to include Air Assault School (receiving his Air Assault badge), Combine Army Service Staff School (CAS3), Command and General Staff College (CGSC), and attended college to receive his first Master's Degree. CPT Gelhardt was then transferred to the 527th Military Intelligence (Counter Intelligence) Battalion, as the Battalion S1 (Chief Administration Officers), in Kaiserslautern, Germany. This specialized unit was a classified unit (that no longer exists) that was in the business of catching spies. While assigned to the 527th MI (CI), Battalion, that unit caught more spies than any other organization within the government. CPT Gelhardt was then selected for a joint service command, as the Commander, Defense Courier Service, Ramstein Air Force Base, Ramstein, Germany. CPT Gelhardt's unit was one of the first units to deploy to the Middle East in support of combat operations for Desert Shield/Desert Storm (DS/DS). After DS/DS, CPT Gelhardt was transferred back to the United States, to Fort Gordon, in Augusta, Georgia where he attended the first Army computer operations functional area (FA 53A) school. At this time, CPT Gelhardt was promoted to Major (MAJ). His next assignment was with Headquarters, Third Army/Army Forces Central Command (ARCENT). MAJ Gelhardt held both positions in Information Technology (Deputy Chief of Staff/G6) and in Human Relations (Deputy Chief of Staff/G1) area. During this assignment, MAJ Gelhardt supported Somalia combat operations, re-deployed to the Middle East several times, and deployed to Egypt in support of the Bright Star exercise. During this time MAJ Gelhardt was awarded the Soldiers Medal, the Army's highest peace time medal for valor, for saving a pregnant young lady from a burning car during a traffic incident. MAJ Gelhardt was promoted to LTC and was assigned to The White House Communications Agency, in Washington, D.C. This book is about LTC Gelhardt's time at The White House. After his assignment to The White House, LTC Gelhardt was assigned to First Army Headquarters as the Chief Information Officer (Assistant Chief of Staff/G6). While at First Army LTC Gelhardt was selected for promotion to Colonel. Mr. Mark Gelhardt retire from the service September 2001.

Colonel Mark Gelhardt continues to give back to his country in the Georgia State Defense Force, Georgia National Guard Auxiliary, as the Chief Information Officer (ACofS, G6) for the state of Georgia.

PREFACE

This book covers the inner workings of The White House, the Presidency, and the hard work of the military members that support the Commander-in-Chief.

The primary reason for this book and telling these stories is so my family and my friends can now know what their dad, husband, and friend was doing for four and half years while at The White House.

Throughout my time at The White House, I learned a lot of classified government secrets. I had to mentally segment the classified from the unclassified information. I had to continually consider what I could tell my wife and family and what I could not tell them about my job.

It was incredibly hard to segment what I could talk about, so I found it easier to just not talk about my work at all. I was not supposed to divulge classified information. Not talking was the safest thing to do, even though this created extra stress in my family life.

I worked with some great people that had "Can do" attitudes, that helped make the long hours, hard work, and stress worthwhile. Your military is supporting your government everyday putting themselves in harm's way every day - don't ever forget that.

I worked with a lot of classified information, I saw a lot of Presidential secrets, I heard a lot of Clinton family issues, and it was hard to know all this information and not say anything. However, I was a professional military officer with a mission to do and I had signed an oath!

Now twenty plus years later, much of what was classified then is no longer classified and is openly available to the public in one form or another. I will not divulge anything in this book that is still classified. Any still classified stories will have to wait for a later time or may never be told.

What I am sharing are some great stories about the inner workings of The White House and some very funny stories about things that happened to me and my friends while working at The White House and with the President.

I was proud to work with the men and women of the Armed Forces that support the Commander-in-Chief. I was proud to do my duty for my country and I hope everyone enjoys the stories that make me smile every time I tell them.

My Time at The Clinton White House

CHAPTER 1

How I got to The White House

I was just about to reach my fifteenth year of military service in the Army and I was trying to decide what to do next in both my military career and in my life! At this point in my life, I still had no idea that I would soon have a job that would affect the whole world. You never know where your path in life will take you. My path took me to The White House standing next to the President of the United States.

FINDING THE JOB

In July 1994 I was working at the Headquarters of the Third United States Army located at Fort McPherson which was in Atlanta, Georgia. Third Army was a large unit commanded by a three-star general and was in charge of all the U.S. Army Forces in the Middle East (Iraq, Kuwait, Saudi Arabia, Somalia, etc.). Lieutenant General John J. Yeosock, who I worked with several times during Desert Shield/Desert Storm (DS/DS), had asked me to come work for him back in 1991. My family and I had moved to Atlanta, Georgia and I had been working at Third Army for the last couple of years. I had been at this duty assignment right in the middle of all the action that was happening in the Middle East, the aftermath of Desert Storm, the conflict

1

in Somalia, and other events in the Middle East. This was a great assignment for an officer of my rank and for this time in my career. I was actively participating in all the current Army activities in the Middle East, but it was time for me to think about what was next in my career and my life.

I was currently the Director of Human Resources for Third Army specializing in military awards, I was in charge of processing all the wartime awards that came from Army units in the Middle East. By this time, the Army had redeployed back from the Middle East. Desert Shield and Desert Storm (DS/DS) was over and there were a lot of wartime awards that still needed to be processed from that action. Also, during this time, the Somalia conflict had started and the US Army was deployed and fighting in that area. With all this work on wartime awards, I had become one of the Army's top experts in this field. I had the honor of processing the two Medal of Honor awards for the conflict in Somalia during the Blackhawk Down event.

It was 1994 and the military was considering drawing down the number of troops on active duty. The cold war was over, the Berlin Wall was down, and we had just won the conflict in Iraq over Kuwait. The politicians thought it was time to cut the military. The military had started offering an early retirement program for qualified officers with more than fifteen years of service, but less than twenty years (the normal retirement time). I fit into this category for early retirement. I had a decision to make; get ready to move my family to my next duty station or take the early retirement. I started debating what to do now with my career and my family.

As I debated what to do next, I looked at my military options, what positions and locations were open and available to me. I had just come out on the promotion list to Lieutenant Colonel (LTC) and knew it would take me about a year before my promotion would happen. Part of my thought process also included the fact that after being promoted I would have to stay in the service for three more years to be able to retire at the higher pay grade of LTC. These were all factors in my decision. How far did I want to go within the Military?

In the military, they move you all the time from job to job, post to post. This was just our way of life, you move and change jobs all the time. In my career, I had rotated between spending half my time in the Information Technology (IT) field and half my time in the Human Resource field. I would have an Information Technology job for twelve to twenty-four months then I would switch to a Human Resource job for the next twelve to twenty-four months. I was currently doing my rotation in the Human Resources field.

Lucky for me, one of my best friends was the Director of Human Resources specializing in the personnel requisitions and assignment fields. It became useful and very helpful to have the right friends with the right connections to help me find my next job in the military.

On the family front, my children were getting older, my son, David, was finishing up elementary school at Braelinn Elementary, in Peachtree City Georgia. My second child, Kristine (Kris) was also in the middle of elementary school at Braelinn Elementary. It was time to start thinking of my family. If I retired we would be staying in a great city (Peachtree City, Georgia) which had great schools, great police and fire, and great amenities. Folks call living in Peachtree City, "Living in the Bubble". We had not long ago purchased our first real home after fifteen years of moving all over the world for the military. I had joined the Peachtree City Fire Department as a volunteer quickly moved up the ranks to become a volunteer officer. We had all made friends and laid down roots in a safe community. We loved living in the bubble, why move?

My question at this point in my life was to retire and stay where I was living in Peachtree City for my family OR to move to wherever the Army needed me next? I started working on my options. What options would the military provide? The military picks your next assignment, they tell you where you are going, however, if you know the Human Resource system you can help influence where the Army sends you.

Thanks to my good friend, I had direct access to the Total Army Personnel System, an automated system that showed all open positions within the Army. I thought I knew the Human Resource system for filling positions and now I had access to that system. I started looking through every open position across the Army, what type of positions, their locations, which units, etc. I thought I knew how to use the system – but I was wrong!

When I looked into the Army automated personnel system; I didn't find any jobs, units, or locations that I wanted. Now What?

I was asking a lot of my friends for their input on what to do and the word got around that I was thinking about getting out of the service. I received a call from an old friend of mine that had worked for me several years before. I had been his Commanding Officer previously and had helped convince this outstanding young enlisted soldier to put in a packet to become a Warrant Officer. I guided him all the way through the process and eventually was able to promote him to Warrant Officer. Now this great soldier was the one calling to help convince me of something.

This call started the change in my life that I would never forget. He heard through the grapevine that I was looking for my next position and had information about two top-notch jobs he thought would be perfect for me. I asked him how he knew of these positions and then found out that thanks to the evaluations I had written for him, he had been nominated and selected for a top-notch job himself. You see, this friend of mine that I had helped out years before was now working at The White House.

My friend was now the Chief Warrant Officer for Human Relations for The White House Communications Agency. He told me of two Lieutenant Colonel positions at The White House, one in the Information Technology field and the other in the Human Resource field. These positions at The White House were news to me, I had already looked in the Army Personnel System for all the open positions and did not find these. I learned that selective nominated positions were not in the Army Personnel System. There was another personnel tracking system for these type of nominated and selected Joint Duty assignments/positions. Joint positions are positions that can be filled by Army, Air Force, Navy, or Marines. I had the pleasure of being in another joint positions previously in my career and was aware that working joint was a little different, but I loved the challenge it brought. With some help from my friend, I was able to locate the joint positions hidden within the Army system.

When I looked into it further and did some research about The White House positions, I found that I did indeed meet all the requirements for the position. As a matter of fact, I met the requirements for both the HR position and the IT position. I now had something I was interested in shooting for and felt it would be worth moving my family to work at the center of the government – The White House!

GETTING THE JOB

I decided to call the people in charge of these special positions at the Pentagon and inquire as to the status of the two open White House positions. I asked specifically about the Information Technology position, which was the job I really wanted. When I talked to the Pentagon office in charge of filling these positions, they informed me that I was not in the top 1% of officers and that they had other more qualified personnel to nominate for these important positions. They were looking for the cream of the crop, the people that knew how to walk on water and looked like recruiting posters. I understood what they told me, I was good, but I was not good enough!

I gave this rebuke from the Pentagon some thought. I agreed that I was not in the top 1% of the Army, but I did think I was at least in the top 10% maybe even in the top 5% if I stretched. I didn't let this hold me back. I did some more research on these positions and tried to find out what this White House job was all about. How to get into a position, how to be nominated? I figured if I couldn't get the Army to nominate me for the job – I would just do it myself! The next question was how?

I called my friend who'd told me about the jobs and asked him how he got nominated and accepted for his position at

The White House. I asked him what he went though and how he made it to where he was now. I asked him how he get nominated. He told me that he may not be in the top 1% of his field, but he did have a Top-Secret (TS) security clearance with special code word access, had worked other joint jobs, and had a great record thanks to me. I learned from this conversation that you didn't really have to be a top 1% but you had to be the right person, with the right skills, in the right place at the right time with joint service background and have a TS clearance.

I had the skills, I had the Top-Secret security clearance, with special code word access. I was due to rotate, I had the right prerequisites, I had been in a joint duty job as the Commander of the Defense Courier Service, having commanded Navy, Air Force, and Army personnel. I knew I had what it takes to do the job.

I asked my friend who had the authorization at his current unit, the White House Communications Agency (WHCA) to ask the Department of the Army, for me? I was told that the position that would do this type of coordination was the person they were trying to hire – the head of their Human Resource team. That is why they wanted to fill this job right away – it was a critical job for the organization.

With the head of HR position open, I gave some thought what I should do and who I should go to? It came to me - if you want to open a door, go to the top and ask the boss (the commander of that military unit). So, I did!

I worked with my friend to get the schedule of the Commander of The White House Communications Agency. I wanted to know when he would be in the office and when his secretary would not be in to answer the phones. I did my research and found out what was in the normal Department of Defense and Department of the Army nomination packets for White House jobs. I collected all the information for a nomination packet and had it ready to go. This was a ton of paperwork I needed. My last five Officer Efficiency Reports (OERs), an official photo, a copy of my officer record brief, and much, much more. Soon I had the packet ready, I had the information I needed and my plan had come together – now I had to execute!

I waited until my friend called and told me that night would be the best opportunity. The secretary for the Commander would not be in and that the Commander just got back from a trip with the President of the United States (POTUS) and would be in his office late catching up on his paperwork.

My friend and I set up a plan to get my foot in the door. Hopefully I wouldn't get my foot cut off and the door slammed in my face – but it was a chance I was willing to take. After all, I could still retire if this didn't work out.

THE CALL

I received another call from my friend at 6:00 P.M. and he told me to call the Commander now. He provided me with the direct dial information to the Commander's personal line on his desk and I called Colonel Jake Simmons, the Commander of The White House Communications Agency (WHCA). He answered on the second ring and I told him that I was Major (Promotable) Mark Gelhardt and that I wanted to come work for him. He told me this was not the way things were done. I told him if he gave me five minutes I could change his mind and better his unit. Amazingly Colonel Simmons gave me five minutes and listened to my pitch. I told him who I was, I gave him a brief background and history of my career and again I told him I wanted to work for him at The White House. He responded that there was a full process to follow and that Department of Defense and Department of the Army are the folks that put together a list and the packets for nominated officer. I told him that I had already tried that route and they did not think I was good enough to nominate. I told him I disagreed and that I was self-nominating. I also told him that I had faxed a completed nomination packet to his personnel fax machine behind his desk while we had been talking. He asked me how I found out what was in the official packet and how I got the forms since I was not officially nominated. He also asked me how I got his phone number and fax machine number. I told him that I was motivated, that I had skills, and that if he hired me he would be hiring that motivation and those skills.

My five-minute phone call lasted thirty minutes and finally Colonel Simmons said he had other matters to attend to and this conversation was over. I thanked him and hung up. That was that – I gave it the good old college try. Now I would wait and see what would happen.

Two days later, I received a phone call from the Department of the Army from an officer I had talked to earlier about nominating me and he was absolutely irate! He was yelling at me up one side and down the other. He asked me what the hell I was doing. I told him I didn't know what he was talking about and could he elaborate. He told me that he got a by name request from The White House to have me come up and interview for possible open positions at The White House. I told him I had no idea how that happened, but my inside voice was yelling "I did it!" I told him that I knew several people that worked at the Pentagon and in Washington D.C. and maybe someone mentioned me. I know he did not believe what I told him because later that day I received a call from his boss, the Chief for the Army team that nominates officers. This General Officer was not polite at all to me, either. He told me that I had ruined my Army career and he would see to it. Then he told me that he didn't know what was going on, but I was representing the Army now and I better do damn good during the interview process. He also told me what my options were if I didn't get this job, none of which appealed to me, but that is what happens when you go over the heads of those in charge of such things.

Next, I received classified orders to report to Washington D.C. the following week. This meant that I couldn't just ask anyone questions to find out more information. When I called the Army and asked how I could go about obtaining further details, you can guess the type of help I received – none! I made my bed, now they were going to let me lie in it.

I didn't know much other than I was going to D.C. and that I was supposed to stay at a specific hotel, reporting to the lobby at 8:00 A.M. Monday morning. Ok, the ball was served and it was in my court. All I could think of was, the door is open, what am I going to do now?

I am a person that likes to be prepared, I always think of the scenarios that may occur. With no information it was very hard for me to be ready and fully prepared. For example, I leave early for the airport, because if I get a flat tire on the way to the airport, I have time to change it and incase I mess up a suit while changing my tire, I have two suits, or don't wear a suit on the trip at all and change later. I always think ahead and am always prepared, what is the primary option, what is the secondary option what is the third?

Here, I was going into a process that I knew nothing about and I didn't have time to do more research and prepare the way I normally would. I got the orders late in the week and had to show up the following Monday. During the weekend, I packed and repacked and tried to think of all that I might need for the coming week. I got a very short military haircut, I had my dress green uniform pressed and measured all my ribbons and badges so they were in precisely the right place. I packed two suits with very conservative ties and shirts. I had everything that I could think of and off to D.C. I went wondering what would happen next. Will this be a new door opened for me changing my life or will I get the door slammed in my face?

INTERVIEW WEEK

Monday morning at 7:00 A.M. I was in the lobby of the hotel in my full-dress green uniform with all my ribbons and badges showing on my chest. I looked like a recruiting poster, cut hair, shaved clean face, and a uniform that fit like a glove. I was ready to put my best foot forward. I was one hour early, I was thinking ok what is next, I am ready, whatever it is. I was psyching myself up for what was next. I thought I was good enough, I knew it, I had nothing to lose. If this didn't work out, I would just retire. I was ok with that.

I stood there in the lobby waiting for whatever was next. I did not sit down because I didn't want my uniform pants to wrinkle and I wanted to look my best. I was walking around the lobby not sitting down and I started to see other sharp looking military type personnel show up in the lobby early, just like me. The people all looked like military posters, short hair, clean shaven, physically fit, all looking better than the average military type. You could just tell what type of people these were, all fast track, confident professionals. But, everyone I saw was in civilian clothes, men in coats and ties, women in business attire. I didn't see anyone that was in a uniform like me?

I knew I did not have enough information and it looked like I was in the wrong outfit. So, I thought I would ask some questions of the military folks I saw in the lobby. I walked up to one person and asked them if they were in the military, they said, "Yes". I ask if they were here on orders to interview for a job. Again, my orders were classified so I was walking a fine line of questions and answers to get the information I wanted, and that I needed. The answers I was getting led me to believe this individual was here for the same reason I was. So, I just asked if they were there to interview for a position at The White House. I was imminently chastised by the person, saying it was classified. I told him I only had one more question to ask. I said I did not understand why he was not in uniform – then the bombshell dropped. He told me he received a pre-interview packet with the events of the week, what to expect, and the uniform for each event and for each day.

I did not receive this information and had no idea what he was talking about and he was not willing to share any more information. Again, we were on classified orders. He did tell me that civilian clothes were the attire for the morning. If I was there for the same reason he was, I was in the wrong clothes. I immediately turned and went back to my room and changed into a suit and tie and rushed back to the lobby of the hotel and instead of being an hour early I was five minutes late. There was a person in civilian clothes at the front door of the hotel calling my name, "Last call Mark Gelhardt," I rushed up and was told to get onto the bus, that I was late and that was not appropriate. I had no good response other than to say, "No excuse, sir!" and got on the bus. In my head, I was thinking, "What a way to start!" I knew I was already behind everyone else for these interviews and that I'd have to play catch up all week long. I also realized that the General from the Pentagon who yelled at me the week before hadn't sent me the briefing packet with the week's event schedule. I don't know for sure if he did this on purpose, but I suspected it was. I had gone around the system and he didn't like that. I realized that all these rock star folks had weeks or months to get ready and I'd had no time at all. This took a lot of wind out of my sails, but I had nothing to lose I would keep pushing forward. I looked around the bus and recognized the same people that had indeed been in the hotel lobby. This was going to be a tough week, I was against the top 1% of military officers and I now knew it, no packet, in the wrong clothes, and now late to the bus. I knew I was going to be behind all week!

There were about twenty-five people in the bus and I didn't know if they were all interviewing for the same job or not. I thought I was up for the challenge at least before this morning's events. Our first stop was to receive our security briefings. We were all read into several Top-Secret programs that we would need to know about throughout the week. We were all briefed into the same program and that meant we could talk amongst ourselves about this process as we were all cleared. Another good thing for me, we all received an updated packet of the week's events. Now I was up to speed about what the schedule of events was going to be. I started to get my self-confidence back.

We started a week of interviews with one person or another and other times with panels of individuals of one type or another. As the days went by, I noticed each morning that fewer people were showing up. By Wednesday we were down to a large van vs. the bus from Monday. People were either asked to leave or dropped out on their own as they found out more about the job. The week went by quickly. We were given a polygraph test. We were interviewed by technical people asking a lot about the technical side of the job. I was interviewed by two technical groups, a Human Relationship (HR) group and again by the Information Technology (IT) group. I found that a little interesting at the time but didn't give it much thought as I didn't know what the norm was for interviews.

We were interviewed by political people, from The White House, Chief of Staff office. Those were some of the most interesting interviews for me as a military member. They asked me my views on abortion, on gun control, if I was a Republican or a Democrat, what I thought of the president, of his policies, of the missions given to the military, and on several other hot button topics. I knew this was coming, after all it was The White House. My answer to all these questions was the same, "I am a military officer. I follow the orders of the officers over me who follow the orders of the elected officials over them." Then I would follow up with "All my political opinions are personal and will be reflected in the privacy of the voting booth. I would not comment on any political issue while in the military and will follow all orders given unless they would bring harm to myself and others, and/or could be considered immoral or against the law." Then the interviewer delved into what I considered to be immoral. Man, these interviewers were really picking at me and I assume the other candidates as well.

During all these interviews I guess I must have said the right things because I was there the next day and the next day. Finally, it was Friday morning and there were only four of us left. I remember talking to a Marine Corps Major, asking her how she was doing and if she was excited about being in the final round. I was amazed by her response to me. She said she didn't want the job and didn't want to work in The White House. She continued by saying that this job would hurt her career and the only reason she was even here was because the Marine Corps nominated her. She felt like she didn't have a choice. I asked her, how come she didn't just bow out during the week, there were plenty of opportunities and many other had done just that. I really liked her answer, she said "It wasn't in her nature, to not do her best. She had to keep pushing to be the best Marine Officer she could be." She continued, "That even though she didn't want to be there and would hate doing the job, she was a Marine and would not pass on a mission that her command sent her on." I love working with military members like this professional Marine Officer. Duty, Honor, Country is a way of life for professional military members. She was living that moto. I would later find out that the Marines I worked with at The White House were some of the most professional and impressive people I ever had the pleasure to know. We did one more round of interviews Friday morning. By noon that day there were only two of us left. The female Marine Officer hadn't made the cut.

There I was an Army Major (promotable) having lunch with an Air Force Lieutenant Colonel. We had changed out of our civilian clothes for this last day and we were in our full dress military uniform. I was in my Army Greens coat and tie uniform, for the Air Force officer he was in his Air Force Blues, coat and tie uniform. This was the first time we wore our full-dress uniforms with all our ribbons and badges. I had a lot of ribbons and badges on my uniform, but so did the other guy. We both looked sharp, I mean recruiting poster sharp. Most of the week we wore civilian coat and tie, most of the folks we interviewed with were in civilian coat and tie. Most everyone introduces themselves with their names and if they were in the military they never gave us their rank. However, you could just tell that half the folks we interviewed with were in the military, the haircut, their style, the way they talked; we had no idea what rank they were, what service they were in, who they really were and how they fit into the job chain of command. I came to find out later that several of the individuals who had interviewed me were senior enlisted members, and some were even junior officers. As it turns out, many of these enlisted and officers would later work for me. For a military job, this was sure a unique way of doing business.

After lunch we were told that we would be reporting to a military board of senior officers for our final interview. We were to be called into the interview one at a time. The Air Force officer went in before me. I had asked questions to get information as to what was going on and I found out that we were the last two officers that were being considered in this round. I knew that there was only one

Information Technology Officer position open. I also found out that they only did rounds of interviews for officers about twice a year. I would either make it or not. As I sat there in the outside office and waited my turn, I started thinking again of my options. What was next for me in life, what door would I have an opportunity to take?

My mind raced, if I got the job when would I move, where would I move, and how would my wife and kids adjust to another Army move, this time to D.C.? Going over all these options actually gave me a headache. Then I started to think ok, what if I don't get the job? Would I really retire – yes, I think I will take the early out and keep the kids in the same place with the friends they had made. My wife and I had made friends too. Peachtree City was a great place to live. We living on the economy in a house we purchased with a two-car garage and I drove up to the Army base. It was like being a civilian. You know not getting this White House job may just be the best outcome after all, what was I doing moving my family again? We had already moved more than a dozen times over a fifteen-year career. Was it fair to move them again? Then I was called, it was my turn. Man, my head was all messed up from thinking about everything and just before I was to be interviewed, talk about really bad timing on my part!

I opened the door, marched into the room stood at attention and saluted the board of officers, specifically the head board member seated at the middle of the table. It was then that I noticed that several of the people that I had been talking to during the week were actually General Officers, all very senior to a little old Major like me. The two-star general that was leading the board returned my salute and told me to have a seat. He started right in and told me that they had decided to offer the Information Technology job to the Air Force Lieutenant Colonel that was just in the room before me. He continued by telling me that the other officer was more technically qualified in IT then I was. Well, I said to myself, "Ok that is that, back to Peachtree City, Georgia I go and into an early retirement."

I stood up and started to salute and said, "Thank you very much for your time." I was ready to go, I had thought through that option and I was ok with it. Just then the one-star General to his right said "Not so fast Major have a seat." Of course, I sat right back down, what did I do wrong, am I going to get yelled at now? To my surprise the Colonel to the left of the Two Star started talking. He said that I had a very interesting career and that I did outstanding during the interview process. They were very impressed with me and that I had a background they could use. I said "But you said I wasn't as qualified as the previous officer in the IT field," he said "That is correct." But then he went on to say that I was a very qualified Human Resource person. I was the only Human Resource person they had seen with the amount of field experience in multiple joint services roles. I had a unique career, I had worked in the Human Resource field in the 82nd Airborne Division, I had worked in Human Resources in a black listed unit the 527th Military Intelligence Battalion (Counter Intelligence). I had been the Commander of a joint command with the Defense Courier Service. I had been in a combat command during Desert Shield/Desert Storm, and so on. They said that the Human Resource people that frequently sent over by the Pentagon are all just straight paper pushers, all they knew was HR, they didn't know the field operational side of the house. They were grade A+ HR people, but they didn't know how to relate to the operators, to understand what field enlisted, Non-Commissioned Officers, Warrant Officers, and Officers needed to do their job. They then said something that would change my life forever. They offered me the Director of Human Resource job at The White House Communications Agency (WHCA).

I thanked them and said "No sir, I really wanted the IT job and even though I am fully qualified for the HR job I didn't really want to do that." I stood up and started to salute again to leave. This time the General said "Not so fast Major sit back down." Of course, I did what I was told and sat back down. I had nothing to lose, I didn't get what I wanted - I lost the IT job and was ready to do option two – early retirement. The General started talking to me and wanted to know why I didn't want to be the Director of HR at The White House. I told him I had done HR on and off throughout my whole career and I knew I was good at it, but that is not what I had a passion for. It is not what I wanted to do for the rest of my life and or career, I wanted to go into IT and that would help me be ready for retirement when that comes. I enjoyed the military life and the service, but I needed to be ready to take care of myself and my family after the service in retirement.

I don't think they knew what to say to me I was being totally open and honest with them. I am not sure anyone had ever turned down such a prestigious job. They were so used to top 1% of officers that were looking to do whatever it took to get promoted and take the prestigious jobs to get there. I think I was someone that was new to them, maybe a breath of fresh air to what they usually got. Now, they started selling me on the job and telling me of the problems they were having in the HR area and that they would like for me to come fix their issues for them. They started talking about the senior people in the HR staff and they mentioned my friend the Chief Warrant Officer that worked on the HR team. I stopped them and told them I knew all about their issues and that I already knew the Warrant Officer and that he and I had been in contact and I was trying to help him already over the phone over the last several months. They kind of looked at each other and said that explained a lot because the HR team was making changes and improving. Now they knew why and how that was happening. I kind of shot myself in the foot because now they were not going to let me go and they told me so. The more direct I was the more direct they were. I am not sure I had ever had a two-star and a one-star general being so direct with me. They were honest and open about issues they had. They finally asked me very directly to come work for them and fix their issues. They needed my help, they wanted my help, it was a good puzzle to fix and I love to fix puzzles. That is what I do fix things and this was something I knew I had the skills to do. How could I say no?

I seemed to be in the driver seat for the first time all week. I had to take a shot and asked them, "If I fix your HR area will you think about moving me over to the IT area?" Here I was trying to barter with generals, but it worked. They said yes, they would think about moving me over to IT if I could fix their HR issues. I was on a roll, so I ask for one more request. I had been working on the largest tank exercise in the world that would happen in Cairo, Egypt in just a few months. This exercise would take place out in the Egyptian desert where tanks have plenty of room to maneuver. I had been working on the "Bright Star" exercise and had spent the past six months getting

My Time at The Clinton White House – Author: Mark Gelhardt

everything ready and it would be very hard to back fill my slot with someone else. I asked if I could delay my arrival to The White House by 4 months, they said "Yes!"

They explained that it would take some time to do the paperwork, to move me, and to get my White House clearance. When you work at The White House in the position I was going into you have to have a very special clearance. A "Yankee White" clearance – the highest clearance in the Department of Defense. Even though I already had a Top Secret (TS) Secure Compartmental Information (SCI) clearance with code word access. I still needed to go through a further process to get my Yankee White clearance. This timing would work well for everyone, I could finish up my current commitment and work in Cairo (which I always wanted to go see the Pyramids) and still go to The White House. This would help the family, giving them more time to finish up, selling the house and doing all the things that is needed to move.

The wheels started turning the ball was rolling. I would now be going to The White House in four months. What did I get myself into? I would soon find out!

BECOMING YANKEE WHITE

I already had a Top Secret, codeword, Department of Defense (DoD) security clearance that I had received for previous jobs that I had. Where I had worked with classified documents at the Top Security code word level and with things like nuclear control keys. I thought I was at the top of the security clearance level – but no! I now found out what it took to get to the highest level of clearance that the government has and become "Yankee White" cleared!

Becoming a Yankee White cleared military member so that I could work at The White House was not an easy task. I filled out a 30-page clearance questionnaire, documenting every place I ever lived since I was born. Luckily, both my mom and I kept everything we needed. We had all the needed addresses in one box or another. I had kept all my old checks from my teen and college years with the addresses on them. My mom had all the addresses where we lived while I was growing up.

Second thing I had to do, is get documents from both my mom and dad about their background. Where they were born, where they lived and information on their relatives. This opened up a lot of discussion around information that I had no idea about. I had never asked and did not realize my mother had been born in a mining camp, in the Philippines, while it was a U.S. colony. Her mother (my grandmother) was working in a mining camp and had married a British Army Officer (my grandfather – who I can never remember meeting). She was not born in a hospital but in a cabin at the mining camp. Learning all this new information about my family started my interest in our family genealogy (which I am still working on).

Almost none of this information I was getting from my family I knew or remembered. My mom never talked about her past, about her life with my father and their divorce. My parents got divorced back when I was four or five I think? I can never really remember my father being in my life. When I filled out all the previous clearance I just said my father was estranged and I did not provide any information, because I didn't know anything. Well that did not work for The White House Yankee White clearance. I took what my mom gave me but I still needed to contact him and get more information for my clearance.

As a side note, I had not meet with or seen my father in many years. When I was growing up I can only remember two times that I had ever seen my father. Once he flew us kids (me and my two brothers) over to Portugal where he was living with his second wife and my step-sister. The second time I remember seeing my father was a time when he was on vacation and came down to South Florida. I remember my brothers and I going over to his hotel and meeting with him, his wife, and my step-sister.

I don't ever really remember having a father and what fathers did or didn't do. My mom did a great job at allowing me to grow up, learn life on my own. I never really knew I was supposed to miss having a father. I knew he existed but I also knew he didn't seem to care about me or what I was doing. I had tried to reach out to him over the years, but these contacts were never very warm and I did not feel wanted. I invited him to my first wedding in the early 80s and he came, but again it was like he was a guest not my family or my father. Now it was fifteen or so years later, I was married and had two children (a boy and a girl) that my father had never met.

Here I was going to a man I didn't really know, that didn't seem to care about me and asking for information that would affected my life and my career. The only things I knew about my father came from my grandfather. My grandfather would tell us some of what my father was doing, but over time even that bit of information about my father stopped. I didn't realize it but my father and grandfather had been estranged for many years after my grandfather got divorced and re-married. My grandfather passed away when I was in my mid-twenties, a long time before I started working at The White House. However, I kept in touch with GranyWee (my grandfather's second wife) for many more years. She would every now and then tell me things about my father that she had heard. She at one time told me that my father had gone to federal jail in Alabama? I never followed that up and had not really cared. If he didn't want to be in my life I would just live with that.

My grandmother (GranyWee) was alive to see me work at The White House and listen to my stories. I even visited her on a couple of Presidential trips up to the Boston area where she lived. I had the honor to lay GranyWee to rest just a few years ago. Bless her soul to heaven, what a great lady. Both her and my grandfather I think of very often, I retell stories of visiting them in New York, going out on their boat, riding the subway, getting free eyeglasses (my grandfather was on optometrist) and more – but that is for another book and other stories.

I finally contacted my father because I had to get some of my questions answered about him, his past, and find out if there may be any issues that may affect me and this great opportunity to work at The White House. GranyWee told me how to contact him and I finally did. I asked him questions about his background, that I need to know. I asked him about his criminal record and didn't really get the exacts. All I got was excuses that he was a scape goat for the company he worked for and that the federal government went after him, because they had to get someone and he was the person. He had been put in jail for a year on federal criminal charges around improper use of money working with foreign governments outside of the United States or something like that.

I thought for sure that my father's actions would impact my clearance, but I no choice but to wait and see. Here was my father a person I did not know, had not met more than a dozen times in my whole life and he may impact my future, my career, my life.

The agency that was handling the background investigation (Personal Security Investigation) called me in more than once and asked me about my relationship with my father, my contact with my father, my knowledge of what he did. They wanted to know if he monetarily used any of his ill-gotten gains to support me. That was an easy answer "No!" Throughout my life as best I know my father never supported me in any way.

I answered all these questions in the security clearance around my dad to the best of my ability. I was very surprised at how in-depth this security clearance process was and then it concluded with a polygraph test. It was a true deep dive into my life from birth through the present day. This process was amazing, I had received some speeding tickets when I was a teenager back in my home town and this process found all those. Since I had not received any tickets over the last fifteen years this did not become an issue.

I don't think a spy could have passed this level of scrutiny. After all that was what this process was all about. On the upside, I now know things I did know before and have great information and background on my family that I can use for my genealogy research.

RUNNING THE WHITE HOUSE from CAIRO

The White House approved my temporary duty to Cairo, Egypt where I worked with the U.S. Embassy and the Egyptian government on the largest multi-national tank exercise in the world, the "Bright Star" exercise, while my security clearance was being processed.

At this point in my career I was a Major (Promotable), which meant I had already come out on the list for promotion to Lieutenant Colonel (LTC). Promotions are done in sequenced order and every month the Army promoted a certain number of promotable Majors off the list. My number was coming up in a couple of months, however the Army wanted me to wear the LTC rank earlier. This process is called "Frocking" when the Army promotes you in rank but does not pay you for the new rank until later. I was frocked to LTC so when I went to Cairo I would be seen by all the other nations as a LTC. Rank is important when you are working with foreign nations. This also meant when I arrived at The White House I would arrive as a Lieutenant Colonel vs a Major.

I deployed to Cairo and worked out of the U.S. Embassy during the buildup phase of the exercise when units were still deploying into the country. Then during the exercise, itself I moved out to a field location at an Airbase just outside of Cairo. My job at the Bright Star exercise was to be the Commander, of the Joint and Combined Visitor Bureau in charge of all the Very Important Persons (VIPs) and dignitaries coming to the exercise.

During this time in Egypt, I held phone calls with the Human Resource staff at The White House. I received my security clearance while I was in Cairo and was able to talk about classified White House information through the equipment available at the Embassy. I would have a staff call in the morning and then again in the evening. I worked very long days for six months working both the Bright Star exercise and with my future job of Human Resource at The White House. All I did was work, sleep and eat (if I had time) for six months. What a grind this was. I should have seen this as an indicator of what my life would be like for the next four years at The White House.

I worked with the current Warrant Officer that helped me get the job and with the other staff at The White House. I was able to hire an Air Force senior non-commissioned officer that I had worked with before. He was a Chief Master Sergeant (CMSgt) that was working at the Pentagon and was able to get his Yankee White clearance and reported to The White House in two months. I worked with the WO and the CMSgt every day. We talked about what the issues were and how to fix them. We had to let some military members go and started our hunt for better personnel to meet our mission. We stream lined how we did HR support, we documented processes, and we cross trained individuals in multiple service areas. We did this work together over a six-month period while I was in Cairo. We fired and hired staff and got a great team together. The WO and CMSgt were working well together and the whole team really got a great rhythm going. Moral was up, service was better, and everyone was happy.

The Bright Star Exercise went off very well during this time. We handled distinguished visitors from multiple countries with outstanding results. I learned quickly how to handled Senators, Congressmen, and heads of states. I would use these skills throughout the next several years at The White House. But as much as I learned about dignitaries there was so much I didn't know and would learn those lessons the hard way at The White House.

THE MOVE

In the military you move a lot that is just part of a military life. With a career that spans over twenty-two-year I moved twenty times. The Gelhardt's knew how to move and when I got back from Cairo, my wife had everything ready to go. While in Cairo we put the house on the market to sell. My wife took care of a lot of this. Being an Army wife is not an easy life, you have to be strong, smart, and willing to do a lot of stuff on your own without your partner. Little did I know that this move to my dream job would cost me my marriage, but in the long run it did.

My wife had the house ready to go, she had done garage sales, paired down our stuff to get ready for the movers and the move. I got back from Cairo and drove up to D.C. I took a week to look at houses, at schools, at where my family would be safe and where we could afford to live. I was able to find a house during that week and put in an offer to purchase with a quick close. How to move as a military member would be a whole other book. What to look for, how to do it quickly and how to not lose your shirt while selling one house in your old duty station and purchasing another house in your new duty station. I will not go into all this but as a family team we made it happen over and over again during my time in the military and we did it again for this move.

We moved to the D.C. area in Jan 1995 and were ready for our next adventure. I had no military sponsor for this move, a normal way to move when you are going into a new assignment. A person would be assigned to help you out and be your primary point of contact at your new location. We were not going to a base where there was a whole infrastructure of support for new members moving into their community. There was no support provided by The White House for this move. They expected you to take care of your family and be ready to go on day one. You were supposed to be the cream of the crop in the military, that meant no hand holding. We were on our own, but we had done this enough and we knew what to do.

I had set up a door to door move with the moving company, having them pack up our house in the Atlanta area and move to the D.C. area without having to off load our house hold goods anywhere. We packed up the old house, went to closing the next day, and then loaded up the car and left Atlanta behind starting our next adventure. We arrived in D.C., closed on the new house and got ready for the moving van to show up. I had everything planned down to the hour, with contingency plans built in. Our family moves were done with military precision. But wait, I did not count on the north winter weather.

We were sleeping on the floor of our new house in sleeping bags on air mattresses. We had some items with us like clothes, cooking utensils, toys for the kids, and a TV. Those things we could fit into our two cars that we drove up. The kids were great it was an adventure, new place, new things to see and do. Our kids were fantastic military kids they had moved before and knew the drill. Go outside and find friends your first day in your new house. Well the weather did not cooperate with my military moving plans. I had plan on rain and cold, but I was not ready for the largest blizzard that D.C. had the year we moved. Not inches of snow but feet of snow. The city was shut down, the roads were shut down, the Interstate was closed for a while. There was snow everywhere and being from the south we didn't even have a snow shovel and the movers were supposed to show up the next morning. Well, I did what any good military member does, adapt, improvise and overcome. I started using cardboard from the boxes that we brought with us to dig out the driveway and the walkway to the front door. I looked so funning trying to do this with a cardboard box top, that my kids were just laughing at me. They on the other had were having a ball playing in the snow. Snow was something they had not seen for some time.

Thank goodness for good neighbors. They took pity on me and came out with his snow blower and not only did my whole driveway and walkway, but they also did a large part of the street after I told him the moving van was coming tomorrow morning.

A new house in a new location with a new job is the military life, but usually you move to military bases where everyone helps everyone because you're in the same situation. I found my new neighbors in this civilian neighborhood to be just as nice and caring and helpful. We cleaned off the street and the drive and we were ready for the movers. The next morning came we were ready, but no movers! The movers said that they could not get from the interstate down the city streets to our house to unload and they would take our stuff to the warehouse. I was calling everyone I could think of to stop this from happening, but a lot of the government and the military support personnel had a snow day off. We didn't get our house hold goods for another two weeks and I had to sign in to my new job the very next Monday.

However, I was ready, I had brought all my uniforms with me in the car, I had everything I needed for my new job and was ready to go. My wife and kids would just have to make do with the sleeping bags and air mattresses for the time being as I headed off to The White House.

CHAPTER 2

My First Week at The White House

Jan 1995 - I was ready for my new job, my new challenge, my new duty station, and the next chapter in my life, or so I thought!

ARRIVING AT MY NEW UNIT

It was Monday morning and time for me to report to my new duty station and take my new job as the Head of Human Resources for The White House Communications Agency (WHCA), part of The White House Military Office (WHMO), in support of the President of the United States (POTUS), the Vice President (VPOTUS), the U.S. Secret Service (USSS), and The White House staff.

I showed up in my Class A uniform (coat and tie with ribbons on the jacket – see bio picture) to sign in on Monday morning at 6:30 A.M. and found out that I could not get into the headquarters building, at the Naval Support Facility Anacostia (now the Joint Base Anacostia-Boiling). I had not been cleared yet, I needed an escort and would have to wait in the guard hut until someone could come get me. The gate guard had my name at least that was a good sign.

I was of course early, I always tell my troops if you're not early your late! The place where I was signing in was the Headquarters Building of The White House Communications Agency. It was a classified facility, it had a fence around the building and the parking lot, with an entry guard building. Guest parking was across the street outside the fence area and walk across the street to the small guard building. The Marine guard in the guard building was behind bullet proof glass. I had seen a lot of Marine Guards before but most guards you don't see openly carrying their rifles. This guard was different he had his M16 rifle over his shoulder and it had a loaded magazine in the weapon. This guard meant business and was ready to protect his station.

Even though the guard had my name on their list for entry into the compound, he told me that I would have to wait until someone could come get me and escort me in. But there was nowhere to sit in this small guard building. This was not a place where someone waited around.

Luckily, I was not the only early bird in this unit. A Human Resource person, who I knew, one of the people that I had been working with over the phone from Cairo came out and escorted me into the compound. The Guard buzzed me through the first bullet proof door into a middle section where I had to go through a magnetometer before they would open the inside door that let me into the compound. What a secure facility, I would later find out why. I would continue to find out unique and classified things for the next several years.

MY NEW JOB - OR SO I THOUGHT

When I arrived the person, who met me told me that I could not start the signing in process until I had a talk with the Commander, of The White House Communications Agency. I was called into the Commanders office and the Commander sat me down and reminded me of what I said in the interview several months ago, that I didn't really want the HR job, that I only took it because they needed me and asked me to. I said "Yes sir, I remember all that." He thanked me for the great work I had done with the HR team for the last several months from Cairo. He told me that I had hired the right staff, I got them on board fast and that the policies and procedures I put in place were having the proper affect. He told me that HR team was running smoothly and was fixed. Again, I thanked him for the kind words, then said "So what does that mean for me if you don't need me to fix the HR unit anymore?" I was a little upset, I had just up ended my family with the move and had changed my whole life for this opportunity. Was this for nothing? My head was going in the wrong direction fast, then the twist came!

The Commander also reminded me of what I said in the interview months before that I didn't want the HR job but I really wanted the Information Technology (IT) job. I said "Yes, I remember that" and then I said, "You told me I was not the most qualified technology person for the job." He said that was right he did tell me that. I thought to myself, "Ok, here it comes!"

He said, "Can you turn around the IT department like you did in the HR department?" I couldn't say, "Yes" fast enough. I was being an ass in the meeting because I thought I was going to get fired before I even got in the door. Now I was excited again, super excited, then another bomb shell dropped. The Commander told me I couldn't be the senior officer in that unit, I couldn't be the Commander. He reminded me that they had just hired someone else to be the Commander, Data Systems Unit (in civilian terms - Chief Information Officer/CIO) and that they didn't want to fire him, he was a great officer, a great technical person, and had an outstanding record.

They asked me if I would be the Deputy Commander, or the number two person in the unit. The Deputy position was really the position that did most of the work with the troops and made most of the decisions, because the Commander was always going to meetings and doing other administrative actions. You know I was ok with that. I had been a deputy before in my career and it had worked out. I had worked for other Commanders my whole military career and I was ok with helping them and the unit succeed. I still got to work in the IT field at The White House, that would be good enough for me. My family wouldn't have to move again, I had a job, it was a good job in the field I wanted. Not the job I was expecting, not the one I wanted, but a good job doing important work, at The White House, supporting the President of the United States.

Yes, I took the Deputy job. I was the Deputy Commander, Data Systems Unit, The White House Communications Agency, part of The White House Military Office, in support of the Commander in Chief (the President). I was a Lieutenant Colonel, working for another Lieutenant Colonel who was the Commander of the unit. This was not a good career move for me if I wanted to advance to Colonel. Having one LTC working for another LTC would be a killer for my career. I was not the commander just the deputy another career killer for a LTC. But, I was ok with this, this job would still be in the IT field at The White House.

I meet my new boss, the Commander of the Data Systems Unit, he was the same Air Force Lieutenant Colonel that I interviewed next too over six months ago. He was a nice guy, you could tell he was a fast tracker (that means he was going places). His father was a General Officer and you could tell he would be one too. He had all the right skills, the right jobs, the right personality, and more. He was going to make General and was moving up fast. As Deputy he gave me free rein to change personnel around, to change policies, to run things and to make things better. We got along great, as a team in command of this unit. We both had our strengths and weaknesses that we used to improve everything about the Data System Unit. We developed the strategic plan on how to upgrade IT at The White House and briefed that up the chain of command all the way to the President and we got it approved. We hired a good diverse group of IT professionals to help us in this upgrade and we moved out to get the mission done.

LEARNING TOP SECRET STUFF

The beginning of the day started out normally, fill out this form, or that form, meeting people, getting introduced to so many people that there is no way you will ever remember everyone's names. The second half of my first day was getting read into (told about) Top Secret code word items and projects. They tell you Top Secret information, then they have you sign papers saying you will go to jail if you divulge this information. Some of the things were fun to learn and validated information to have. Some of the things I had already guessed about. Some things I didn't want to know about and wish no one had told me. Classified information is a two-sided sword. On one side you now know the truth, the facts, and have the knowledge, on the other side you know the truth, have the facts and wish sometimes you didn't have that knowledge. Being read in and told about some Top-Secret information can be a very heavy burden. If you are not old enough, mature enough, or wise enough to understand what you now know and how it can affect your country, being read on can be a life changing event.

I had started drinking from the fire hose of knowledge. Everything came fast and furious and I had to segment things that I could tell my wife & family and things I could not, the unclassified to the classified. I mostly didn't talk about the what was going on at the office. It made it easier to keep the classified information from coming out of my mouth. One of the reasons I am writing this book and telling these stories, is so my family and friends can now learn some of the things their dad, husband, and friend did for four and half years while at The White House. I hope everyone enjoys the stories that make me smile and show you the inner workings of The White House, the Presidency, and the hard work of the people that do this job.

It has been over twenty years from the time I was at The White House, many of the things I learned that were classified in the 90s are no longer classified. An example of Top Secret information was the congressional bunker under the Broadmoor Hotel. This was Top Secret, it was about the continuity of the government and no one was supposed to know until 1992 when a reporter released information about its purpose and location. Well now a day everyone knows about it, there has been a Public Broadcasting Services (PBS) special about it, and people can now take tours of the facilities. My daughter and I have even driven up there and toured the bunker ourselves. Things change over time; classified material gets unclassified or gets out in the open so the public knows about it. I have taken great pains in this book to make sure I do not say anything that is still classified or not known to the public already. I guess there are some things I will take to my grave that I will never be able to share with my family or friends. But I am ok with that, that is what I signed up for, that is what being a soldier is all about, following your orders until you die.

THE 18 ACRES (THE WHITE HOUSE GROUNDS)

Things happen fast at The White House, no time to waste it was day two and they were sending me over to The White House. I had spent day one doing all the paperwork to get signed into the unit, getting read onto all the Top-Secret programs, meet my boss and the team that were working for me. But now it was day two and no time to get comfortable. We were a high-speed unit and you were expected to keep up with the pace or get left behind. I had been told to take the shuttle from Anacostia were our headquarters building was over to The White House. I was told one of the guys on the shuttle would help me out and take me to the place on The White House grounds where I needed to go. I had been told that the appropriate attire for The White House grounds was a coat and tie, because the politicians did not like to see all the military members in their uniforms around The White House. This was my very first indicator of the way the military members would be treated during our duties supporting The White House.

I got on the shuttle from the White House Communications Agency Headquarters over to The White House. This was the first shuttle of the day. There was one other individual on the shuttle with me other than the driver. I was all set he would show me what to do and where to go, after all, that was what I was told yesterday. We were driving over to The White House and I told the other passenger that I was a new person and could he help direct me over to the badge office at The White House and escort me through the process. He said he was sorry but he was not going onto The White House grounds he was coming off shift and was just taking the shuttle to the Metro to catch the subway home. At that time, the shuttle stopped and this guy got out. He tried to explain to me where to go, he did his best but The White House grounds are big. The grounds consist of the Presidential Mansion (The main building), the East Wing, the West Wing, the North Grounds (and what is under it) and the South Grounds (and what is under it), and the Old Executive Office Building (OEOB). The folks that work at The White House call the whole complex "The 18 Acres."

I would have many, many hours to walk the 18 Acres, to explore the grounds, like very few other people every would. For example, I ate my bag lunch in the Rose Garden one day, but now I am getting ahead of myself. This was my very first time on the 18 Acres and I did not have a clue as to where to go and who to see to get my badge. But I would figure it out, I was selected for this duty because I was smart and a go getter. After all I found the job on my own, I made the call on my own to get the job, and now I was here on my own getting my White House badge. I would figure it out.

I was on The White House grounds for the first time. My head was swelling with self-importance. I must have looked like my head was four sizes bigger than my body. I had arrived, I was working at The White House! I was at the top of my career and my life. I was finally somebody! It's funny how many times I thought that, just to be put back in my place by events that happened to me. You have to keep your head on straight when you get to a place of power, when you get to the point you think you are someone. It is so easy to get carried away, I was a normal person, that had a great opportunity, I put my pants on the same way as everyone else. Ok maybe I had some skill sets that got me to where I was, but I always want to remember to try and stay humble. Because if you don't humble yourself, life will do it for you.

One of my many times at the White House

The shuttle driver dropped me off at the south lawn drop off area and I got out – ok now what? I had arrived and there was The White House – and there was a large black metal fence all around it? What do I do now? I followed the fence around to the left to where I finally found a United States Secret Service (USSS) guard gate. I asked one of the uniformed Secret Service agent, which was the entry gate for newcomers that I needed to be at to sign in and be escorted to get their badges. He said I was in the right place and for me to provide my photo ID. I was happy to find my name was on his list and he let me into the building through the first bullet proof glass doors into the alcove area. I signed in and then went through the magnetometers into the inner area of the guard booth. I was given a visitor's badge and was told I would not need an escort because I had already been cleared and that I could just go to the badge office and get my new badge on my own. The uniformed Secret Service agent I was talking with was my first of many that I would work with throughout the next four years. He was professional, nice, friendly, and was a great indicator of the other agents I would work with. I have nothing but great things to say about these fine professional men and women that put their lives on the line every day in support of this great nation.

I was inside the fence now and the Secret Service agent gave me the room number of the badge office and told me that the badge office was in the Old Executive Office Building (OEOB). I was off, went into the building and found out that the office numbers were in no order at all. This building was so old and re-used and changed around for every administration that nothing was easy to find. But that was ok I was on the 18 Acres inside the fence, I had finally made it.

THE WHITE HOUSE BADGE

I eventually found the office by going up and down every hallway reading the door signs and the numbers until finally I found the right place. I received my White House Badge and was told that this was an "All Access" badge. I also received an "All Access" pin to put on my jacket. I was able to go anywhere, walk up to anyone, even the President without being stopped by Security Service or the staff, with this badge and pin. My badge & pin had great power, and I remembered the old adage "with great power comes great responsibility." I was learning that this job was even more stressful then I thought. I had the access and power to affect lives, affect our country and to do things I could never image in my wildest dreams. Be careful with power, be careful will all access, it can get you in trouble and yes it did get me in trouble a couple of times!

My second day at work in my new job and here I was at The White House with my "All Access" go anywhere badge. I was supposed to have a White House Communications Agency person to show me around, but he was busy right then. I was told to take this time and get familiar with the grounds basically, go exploring on my own for an hour or so and then come back. Then he would give me a tour of our work spaces and educate me on the knowledge that I would need for my job.

I went exploring on my own and walked around the Old Executive Office Building (OEOB). I walked through all the hallways and looked at all the pictures on the walls and the door signs. Some of the door signs you could tell were new and were made in the last several years. Also, you could see some of the signs that were on the walls from when the building was first built, carved in the marble. The current Old Executive Office Building (OEOB) was built in 1871/88 when it housed the State, War, and Navy Departments. The military departments moved out of the OEOB to the Pentagon after its construction in 1941/43. The State Department moved out of the OEOB to its current Headquarters in the Harry S Truman building in

1943, when other parts of the War Department moved out of that building to the Pentagon. Then the Executive branch took over the OEOB for its ever-expanding staff and office space needs. This was a neat bit of history that I was teaching myself just by walking around and reading all the signs and looking at the pictures. This was great history to learn, I felt like I was in a museum. I really enjoyed it and highly recommend everyone to learn about how our government grew over time.

It was at this time I left the OEOB and walked across the road between the OEOB and the West Wing of The White House. I was going to walk the halls of the west wing to read its signs and then do the same on the East Wing of The White House. I had procured a copy of a visitor map of The White House grounds and was looking at it as I was walking. I was not really paying attention to my surroundings. I tried to open the door to the bottom level of the West Wing and I could not get it open. Then I noticed a swipe badge security feature and I swiped my badge and then pulled on the door. When I tried to open the door before, it didn't move, so I guess I pulled on it to hard this time. The door swung open way to fast and I hit a young lady behind me with the door. I hit her so hard that I knocked her down on the ground. I said, "I was sorry for that" and didn't think much of it until later that day.

I explored the full White House grounds, the West Wing, the East Wing, and some of the underground areas. The White House has a flower shop and wood working shop under the front portico, a bowling alley under the fountain on the North Lawn and much more to explore. I was exploring things, I will not say where on the grounds but I noticed a door that did not look right or the right place. It was semi-hidden and out of the way. I didn't see any signs and/or didn't notice anything out of the ordinary, so I opened the door with my badge and as soon as I did I knew this was not the right thing to do. I was met very quickly by some nice Secret Service agents that asked me what I was doing and where I was going and why I was there. The agents saw my badge and saw it was an all access badge and I could go anywhere. However, I had opened something I should not have, that was obvious. The Secret Service agent was surprisingly nice, he knew I was a new person and cut me some slack. Here I was in the wrong place doing something that was irregular. I wondered if I had already messed up my new job on my first day.

Finally, I hooked up with the person that was to show me around the grounds. He was telling me what to do and what not to do, how to act around the big wigs and providing other knowledge transfer to the new guy, me. When he saw Chelsie Clinton, the first daughter to the President, he pointed her out to me. It was just then that I realized who I had knocked to the ground earlier that day, it was Chelsie Clinton. I had mentioned the event with Chelsie earlier that day when I knocked her down. He told me that he would have to report the incident/event I told him about up the chain. All interactions with VIPs had to be reported. The worse thing was to have the Clintons ask our bosses about something and our bosses not know what they were talking about. This event would be reported and as it turns out I would never here the end of this throughout my career at The White House. As a matter of fact, it played nicely in to the first practical joke planned on me during my time there. That's a great story you will read later.

Here it was my first day at The White House, I had knocked the President's Daughter on her backside, I had set off an alarm and was in a place I should not have been. I was sure my time at The White House would be short lived.

THE BAT PHONE - AT HOME

The wife and I knew accepting The White House job meant making some (or many) sacrifices and that it would change our home life. These changes started right away that first week on the job. Because of my job I had to be available to talk to people and make decisions about work items twenty-four hours a day, seven days a week, 365 days a year and there was no way I could drive into the office at all hours. We had purchased a home in the Lakeridge, Virginia, an area south of the D.C. beltway. This was the best place for the quality of life for my family, very good schools for my kids, and was affordable. We had purchased the house more for the family then me, knowing that I would be working a lot of hours and be traveling a lot. We wanted safety and security for the family and a house that my wife and kids could be happy in. We had great neighbors they had already warmed up to us as soon as we moved in by helping with the snow removal.

As we were setting up the house, the phone company came to my house to put in the private secure military telephone line. Our new house had a home office space on the first floor, I knew I would need a home office. We were ready for the phone company and put the military line into the home office. I came home from the office with a Secure Telephone Unit third generation (called a STUIII) to use for my home office. This phone was a special military phone that allowed people that used it to talk encrypted to anyone else on the other end that had a similar device and the same type of encryption keys.

STUIII see the key in the upper right that could be removed

The phone unit was not classified by itself, it was the key that you put into the phone that was the magic. You called someone normally by dialing a normal telephone number then you tell them that you want to go secure and you both turn your keys in the phone at the same time. The phone sends some signals back and forth and you can tell what level of security you can talk about, by what the security level that is showing on the display of the phone on what type of key the other person has. My key was a top-secret code word key and it would ask the key on the other end what level of encryption it was and then show the highest level that both keys could talk at on a small display on the phone. Even though the STUIII phone was at home in my den all the time. I kept the encryption key with me at all times.

I had to explain to my wife and kids that no one was to use this special phone but me. I told my kids this was like the "Bat Phone" and that only Daddy could use it. I did several test calls with the phone, let my kids see what it sounded like, how it worked, things like that. The phone had several direct dial buttons, I set up a test period with The White House switch board. I let my kids push those direct dial buttons and let The White House switchboard pick up and answer as they normally would. I took the mystery out of the Bat Phone and I don't think my kids every touch the phone the whole time I was in the house. The kids knew dad's job was important, they understood that and they were great about understanding the rules. Great kids!

It was good for me to have this phone in the house so I would not always have to drive to D.C. to do business, that was the up side. The down side is I would get way too many calls on that phone over the years. It would be a sore spot for my wife when it rang at night or on the weekends. But that was the job, always being on call all the time every day.

Because I had a home office with a STUIII phone enabling me to talk about top-secret items at home, we had to have our house swept for bugs on a recurring basis. I never told my wife or kids about the sweeps. I always made an excuse and got them out of the house and had the sweeper team come when they were gone. If my wife had known that we had strangers in our house sweeping it for bugs it would have just been another point of contention with my wife about my job.

LEARNING MULTIPLE JOBS - AT THE SAME TIME

When you join The White House Communications Agency (WHCA) you don't just get one job you get several. By this time, I knew then I would be the Deputy Commander of the Data System unit. That was my full-time job, or what we would call my "Day job," the job I was hired to do. But, when you get assigned to WHCA you have to do many different jobs to keep the mission and The White House going. After all you are there, you are cleared, you have the access, and you were one of the cream of the crop of the military.

I found out that my actual day job as the Deputy Commander for Information Technology at The White House took second and sometimes third place to several other types of jobs that I would have to do. I found out that one of the other jobs I would have to do is being the Presidential Communications Officer (PCO). The PCO position provides the President a signal point of contact for communications needs. You would go everywhere the President went, you would travel both to in town events (i.e., fund raiser, speeches, to the capital, etc.) being in the motorcade, or to out of town or out of country events (i.e., fund raisers, speeches, bi-laterals, Summits, State visits, etc.). Sometimes you would travel with the President, sometimes you would travel to those locations before the president and set up communications for his visits to a location.

A PCO has to be with the President twenty-four hours a day, seven days a week, 365 days a year. I had to sleep at The White House about every other week when I was pulling PCO duty (No I didn't sleep in the Lincoln bedroom). A lot of the stories that I provide in this book are from when I was doing my duty as the PCO. This was the job that gave me the greatest access and contact with the President, his family, and with The White House Staff.

THE BAT PHONE RINGS

I made it to the end of the first week. I didn't get fired yet! I was all processed in, I had been read into all the top-secret programs, I received my White House badge and PIN and had spent time at The White House learning the grounds and the ropes. I had my family set up, unpacked with the kids in school. I had my home office set up with its Safe for classified materials and with the STUIII phone in my office. I had been drinking from a fire hose big time for the first full week. I was trying to learn as much as I can about my primary job doing Information Technology for The White House. I was also learning about my secondary job of being a Presidential Communications Officer (PCO). It had been a long week and I was ready for a much-deserved weekend, then the Bat Phone rang!

This was the first time the STUIII phone rang. Even though the STUIII phone was in my office on the first floor, I had the ringer turned all the way up so you could hear it from anywhere in the house. It woke me up, I jumped out of bed and went downstairs to my office to answer it. I answered the phone and the man on the other end said "Colonel Gelhardt, your plane will be an hour late." I was a little groggy from being woken up after all it was about 5:30 A.M. or so on a Saturday morning and I wasn't expecting anything. I asked him to repeat the message and he told me the same thing. I asked him to explain the message to me a little more in depth, just what was he talking about, who was he, why did he call me? I found out that I was supposed to be the Officer in Charge (OIC) of a Presidential equipment flight for The White House Communications Agency (WHCA) that was leaving out of Andrews Air Force base at 7:00 A.M. and that the flight would now not take off now until 8:00 A.M. At this point I woke up my wife and told her to start packing for me. She asked me what to pack and I said just one of everything and to do it super-fast. I told her I wanted to be out the door in ten minutes or less. I had no idea I was supposed to be on a plane this morning for something. I didn't know what was going on, but in the military missing a movement (or a trip) is a court-martial offense. I was not going to miss this plane even if I had no idea what this was about. I made a second phone call to The White House Communications Agency twenty four-hour operations center and asked them if I was scheduled for movement today. They told me the same thing as the White House Airlift Operations guy told me, but they filled in the blanks a little more. I was added at the last minute as a PCO observer for the trip and that I was to just Observe the trip and use it as a learning trip. The Airlift Operations center called me since I was the most senior person on the manifest and they thought I was the Officer in Charge (OIC) of the mission. This is typical military protocol to expect the most senior person to be the OIC, even though I was not for this particular trip since I was just an observer. The WHCA operations center then asked me didn't anyone tell me during the week when I was in processing? I really didn't know? I couldn't remember anyone saying anything about travel and about being an observer. All I knew is I wouldn't miss this flight, thank God it was delayed an hour. Did I mention that I lived about an hour away from Andrews Air Force Base where the flight was going to take off from?

My wife had me packed in ten minutes. I don't know what she put in my bag but she handed me a bag and out the door I went. I had put on my Class A military uniform (Jacket and tie, with all the ribbons) and I jumped into the car and headed down the interstate doing about 90 to 100 mph towards Andrews Air Force Base. I wasn't worried much about the police. I had a White House badge and would be able to talk my way out of a ticket, or at least I hoped so. I was burning up the road and got to the main gate of Andrews Air Force Base in record time. Then I realize that Andrews Air Force Base is a big place. I wonder where I would have to go to meet my team? I figured we would be at the flight operation center – the main airport type building on a base, were VIPs come and go. I drove past that area and didn't see any movement. It was about 6:45 A.M. on a Saturday morning and I didn't see anyone up on the base anywhere. I had drove like a bat out of hell to get to the base and now I was lost trying to find out where I was supposed to be on this large Air Force Base. This was the mid-90s and cellphones were not everywhere, I didn't have a cellphone so I would have to stop to call the WHCA operations center and ask. As I drove around looking for a payphone to use or an open building, there weren't any I could find. I was losing time fast. I drove back to the front gate to talk to the gate guard. I asked him if he knew of any flights getting ready, he said "No." I then asked him if he knew where the special flights in support of The White House usually flew out of? He said, "That information was classified information." Shoot, I was screwed or so I thought. But then this nice young kid that was the gate guard told me if I drove down the street took a left at the only hanger that did not have a number or name on the side of it, I may find what I was looking for.

Secret information has a tendency to get out even if you don't want it to. This guard knew exactly where The White House missions flew out of. He knew that the unmarked hanger was something special. He helped me out and I headed down the road to the unmarked hanger. I got there and noted all the cars in the parking lot. This was different than the other hangers that didn't have any cars. I felt a hood or two of the cars and they were hot. This was the place, but the building doors were locked.

I grabbed my bag, went to the fence and climbed up and over in my class A uniform (Coat and tie). That must have looked funny, but I got on the other side and walked into the hanger from the flight line side. There was the unit loading equipment on pallets. The non-commissioned officer in charge was the first one to see me and he pulled me aside and said sir, "We don't travel in military uniform, we travel in civilian work clothes." Another learning moment for me, as this was a classified mission, we didn't want to stand out. I had made another newbie mistake. I went into the bathroom and changed. My wife had done a good job at packing for anything when I opened up the suitcase and saw what she put in there. I changed clothes and was ready to started my first trip with The White House Communications Agency. By the way, I had ten minutes to spare before we started loading on the aircraft. I did not miss movement and I was on my way to my first trip in support of the President.

CHAPTER 3

Military Support to The White House

Our founding fathers saw the U.S. Military as an honorable and dedicated organization that would have a pivotal role in our democracy. The military is tasked to ensure the continuity of government of our elected head of state, the President. The military is the organization that makes sure that if the elected head of state dies that the next elected official retains the power to run the government.

MILITARY SUPPORT TO THE COMMANDER-IN-CHIEF

My job at The White House was under the White House Communications Agency (WHCA). Most of the stories in this book are about the Communications and Information Technology support to the President. However, I soon found out that there were many other military units that worked at The White House and that is what this chapter is all about.

Most people would be very surprised at the number of military members that support The White House, the President, the Vice-President, The White House Staff, the US Secret Service, and the National Security Agency. Almost all (with a few exceptions) of the military that support the Executive Branch wear civilian clothes both on and off The White House grounds. Both for in town events and when traveling on the road in support of the President.

As you learned in the first chapter you have to be selected and nominated by your branch of service (Army, Air Force, Navy, Marines, Coast Guard) to work at The White House. As you read in Chapter One, I went around that process. However, the selection process is very in-depth for most people. It is considered a great honor to be chosen as a military support member to the Commander-in-Chief. The positions at The White House are very sought-after positions for a person's military career, especially an officer that wants to make the higher grades of Colonel or General.

This is not only because you are working at The White House in support of the Commander-in-Chief, but most of these positions are "Joint Duty" positions. This means you can get credit in your military records for working with other services. If an officer wants to get selected for Colonel (or Captain in the Navy) he or she must have at least one joint duty position (if not more). There is a policy that states that all flag officers (General/Admirals) must be joint duty qualified before they can be promoted to that senior of a position.

I cannot state enough that I worked with some of the most professional, dedicated, and loyal Soldiers, Airmen, Sailors, Marines, and Cost Guardsmen I have ever had the pleasure to serve with while at The White House. These people were the best of the best, of the people that could pass the security back-ground clearance. I know there were other good people in the service I even tried to get a few of them hired onto my teams at The White House. But, no matter how good you were, you had to be able to pass the rigorous background and security checks or you could not work at The White House. The White House had the best

the services could provide, that could be cleared at Top
Security Yankee White level.

CIVILIAN CLOTHES VS MILITARY UNIFORMS

As a member of the military in support of The White
House, we were told that we needed to blend in on the 18
Acres. We were told not to wear our uniforms on duty but
instead to wear suits (coats and ties) on the 18 Acres.
There were a few exceptions of the no uniform policy, like
the Marines that stand outside the doors to the West Wing,
the Military Aides, and a few others special occasions like
a promotion or awards ceremony.

Because of the civilian clothes policy, duty at The White
House made military members eligible for a special
military civilian clothes paid allowance. However, this
civilian clothing allowance was all messed up, some of the
services provided it, some services didn't. Some services
gave the allowance to enlisted but not officers. Some
services gave higher amounts then other services, and again
some services don't give you anything. This became an
issue within the ranks of those folks that had to purchase
clothes out of pocket. As an Army Officer, I did not
receive any type of clothing allowance. I would however,
have to wear suits every day while on duty at The White
House. Because of what we do away from The White
House you could really mess up your clothes. We would
have to set up communications and automation at every
location we went to, that meant moving equipment, setting
up equipment, pulling cables, and more. I would mess up
about one suit every other month doing this work on the
road. I started buying suits with three or four pair of pants

so when I ruined one pair of pants that suit jacket could still be used with a second pair of pants.

THE WHITE HOUSE MILIATRY OFFICE (WHMO)

All the military that support The White House are controlled and managed by the White House Military Office (WHMO). The WHMO offices are on the second floor of the East Wing of The White House. This provides the WHMO Director with direct access to the Chief of Staff in the West Wing. WHMO is a sub-unit of the Executive Office of the President. The WHMO Director is a political appointee that oversees the Department of Defense assets supporting the Commander-in-Chief (the President). The WHMO Director ensures that requirements are clearly communicated to the all the different military units that support The White House and that these units meet the highest standards of Presidential quality.

The Director position at WHMO comes with the title "The Honorable Mr. or Mrs." When I was working at The White House we went through a couple of political appointee Directors. They may have understood the politics of The White House, but most of them did not have a clue about the military. They had idea how the military did business, how professional we were, and what we would and would not do to fulfill our mission. In most cases the military knew what we were supposed to do better than the politicians. WHMO oversaw a wide array of military assets that accomplished a multitude of missions in support Executive Branch. Both in the unclassified and classified areas. Most of the unclassified units and missions can be found on the web in a google search. These areas include; food service (The White House Mess), Presidential Transportation (The White House Transportation Agency & the Presidential Airlift Group), Medical support (White House Medical Unit), Camp David Support, Bunker Facilities Support, The White House Sentries, Military Aides, Communications/Information Technology services (White House Communications Agency).

I will not talk at all about the classified support structure and the classified missions, but one can only imagine areas that the military may play a role in.

THE MILIATRY AIDES

Military support to the President predates the construction of The White House and originated with General George Washington Aide-de-Camp, whose role as a Personal Aide to General Washington continued when he was elected President. Today we still have Military Aides (MilAides) to the President. There is one military aide for each service (Army, Air Force, Navy, Marines, and Coast Guard). These roles carry a wide variety of responsibilities, from their most important, which is critical military command and control missions to ceremonial duties at Presidential events. These individuals are tasked with carrying the President's emergency satchel, one of the most important military duties that any military member could have.

I interacted with the Military Aides on a daily basis. I got to know them very well as they got to know me. The

Military Aides changed in and out of this job every two years. When the new Military Aides came into someone had to train them and several times that someone was me. I felt honored to have the duty to train the Military Aides, plus it was a lot of fun. The Military Aides had one of the most important missions of any military member at The White House.

It is common knowledge that the Military Aides carry the President's emergency satchel. It was more like a small suitcase or a very large briefcase vs a satchel. The emergency satchel/briefcase is most commonly called "The Nuclear Football." The Military Aides carry the football all the time, everywhere, and they are always with the President. Carrying the football is one of the most important parts of their duties but is not their only duty.

There were a lot of things in that briefcase, some highly classified items, but a lot of non-classified things too. Some of the things the President asked the MilAide to carry just make me smile to think of. The President wanted a soda on the golf course, the MilAide had one in their case. The President wanted to hand out some little nick knack from The White House the MilAide had one in their brief case. You name it tissues, lip balm, snacks, all sorts of things. The President used these official Military Aides doing one of the most important mission at The White House, as a personal servant. I just had to shake my head at this.

The military aides had a lot of additional duties over and above being next to the President with the football. These service members did not have a personal life for two years. They worked ungodly hours both at The White House and on the road. They worked so much that these five officers had their own office on the second floor of the West Wing next to the WHMO office. The Military Aide office had an absolutely huge clothes closet. They had two of everything in that closet from civilian golfing clothes and civilian running clothes to full dress uniforms and mess dress uniforms. These guys would be asked to participate in everything that the President did, with no time to go home and change. One of the Military Aides had to be with the president twenty-four hours a day, seven day a week, 365 days a year (24/7/365), at The White House, at in town events, on the road with the president, on HMX1, or on AF1. The President could not go anywhere without a military aide with the football in close proximity. They would work back to back twenty-four-hour duties all the time. Several of the Military Aides were married but would never get home to see their wives. Sometimes the only time they would see their wife's is when the wife would come into the office to visit with them.

I will talk in Chapter 5 about the team of four that are always had to be with the President 24/7/365. I held a position as the Presidential Communications Officer (PCO) which put me in the same position as the Military Aide. We both had to be with the President 24/7/365. Which is one of the reasons I have so many stories to tell about my time at The White House.

A great friend of mine Lieutenant Colonel Robert "Buzz" Patterson, USAF (Retired) wrote a book about his time as a

Military Aide at The White House. I was at The White House at the same time as Buzz and help train him into his position as a Military Aide. If you enjoy my book and stories about the Clinton White House you may want to read Buzz's book titled, "*Dereliction of Duty*", "The eyewitness account of how Bill Clinton compromised America's national security." Buzz's book has a much different perspective and is much more political than mine. But I still highly recommend his book to get another perspective about the President and the support to the President.

THE WHITE HOUSE MEDICAL UNIT

The White House Medical Unit (WHMU) was established in 1945. WHMU is one of the sub-units under The White House Military Office (WHMO) and is responsible for the medical needs of The White House. The unit provides medical care to the President, the Vice President, their families, and international dignitaries visiting The White House.

The WHMU is led by a Director/Doctor, who typically also serves as the Physician to the President. The Physician to the President is chosen personally by the President. While I was at The White House the physician to the President was Dr. (Rear Admiral) Eleanor Mariano. I got to know the medical staff of the Medical Unit very well as they were always with the Military Aide and myself, twenty-four hours a day, seven days a week, 365 days a year.

There was always a medical person on-site with the Presidential support team.

The medical unit includes active-duty military physicians as well as several physician assistants, registered nurses, and medics. Under implementation guidelines for the twenty-fifth amendment to the United States Constitution, the WHMU Director is the primary official responsible for advising the President's Cabinet on the ability of the President to discharge the powers and duties of the office.

In addition to direct care duties as mentioned, the Medical Unit is responsible for all medical contingency planning for The White House and its key personnel. This includes preparing for every Presidential or Vice-Presidential trip by developing medical contingency plans, including the identification of hospitals and other facilities at which medical care could be provided. The goal is to ensure that the President is never more than twenty minutes away from a hospital with a Level 1 trauma center. If this is not possible, then WHMU ensures that a military helicopter is nearby, kept in instant readiness to evacuate the president to an appropriate hospital.

The White House has a medical office on the ground floor of the main building. This office is closed to the public so you don't see it on the open tours. I would describe The White House office as an urgent care center on steroids. It has a crash cart and other equipment to make it a special needs center. Also, Air Force One contains a full surgical suite with operating table, two beds, resuscitation equipment, various medical monitors, and a full pharmacy.

Lastly in every motorcade there is always an ambulance. All these medical items are run and maintained by The White House Medical Unit.

The medical unit personnel were always along with the Military Aide and myself every day. We worked and traveled a lot with the medical units setting up out of town and overseas locations. I worked with the Medical staff to make sure we had communications at every location they needed to include all the Trauma centers we used.

THE WHITE HOUSE MESS

The White House Mess, was established in 1951 and has been run by the Navy ever since. The White House Mess consists of three small dining rooms located in the basement of the West Wing portion of The White House, next door to the Situation Room. This exclusive dining facility is decorated with handsome wood paneling, nautical trim, and ship paintings. The largest of the three dining rooms seats about 50 people at a dozen tables adorned with elegant table linens, fresh flowers, and official White House china. During the work week, The White House Mess is widely used by senior staff. Breakfast and lunch are served in the Main dining room under the West Wing.

I don't know why but out of all the times I was at The White House I never eat at The White House mess. I think it was just because of timing. I never had time to just sit down and eat a meal. I was always on the go doing something and I always had something to eat with me. If I had to do it all over again, I would have had a couple of sit down meals at the mess. Maybe if I ever get invited back to The White House?

THE SITUATION ROOM

The Situation Room is in the Basement of the West Wing right across from The White House Mess. This small area does a lot of work twenty-four hours a day. The National Security Agency (NSA) provides staff for this area, but so did my team. As the Commander of the Data Systems Unit for the White House Communications Agency. My team provided communications and data support within the Situation Room. My team had a space in this area where we could provide our support, to include paper communications from many locations. We could also make classified copies of items for hard copy briefings.

The Situation Room area is actually several rooms. The biggest of the rooms is the Presidential Briefing room. This room was set up with secure communications to the State Department, to selected embassies, to the Pentagon, to selected agencies and to several other classified locations. The Situation Room is much smaller than most people would think it would be. It was only the size of a small two-bedroom house with many people working on top of each other. Space was always at a premium.

I thought it was funny that the door of the Situation Room had a name plate to the area that said "Situation Room" right on the door. Here was the most classified place in The White House behind the Oval office and there was a sign on the door telling you exactly what it was.

The door has a camera on it and you have to buzz to get in, show your badge at the person inside and be buzzed in the door. You came into a small inner hallway where your badge would be checked and you would sign in. The door for the Presidents briefing room was on the left so folks that didn't really need to come all the way in to the working area would be directed into the briefing room. The other people that were authorized could pass this area and move around to the back side of the situation room where all the work was done and all the communications took place. This is where my guys worked.

I ran a 24/7/365 team that worked in this area that provided hard copy classified material to The White House and the NSA. I ended up going to the Situation Room almost every other day as I checked on my people and their mission. When I spent the night at The White House I always stopped by and checked on my night shift.

THE BUNKER

It has been well documented in open source records that The White House has a bunker. President Franklin Roosevelt constructed this bunker during World War II. The bunker which can withstand a nuclear weapons attack is under the East Wing of The White House.

Back when I was at The White House much of the information about the bunker and its capabilities was still classified. But the events of 9/11 open up the knowledge of the Presidential Emergency Operations Center (PEOC) within the bunker along with other capabilities. You can just look at Wikipedia now and see a picture of the President and his staff in the PEOC. Information that was classified in the mid-90s is now in open source about the bunker.

As the Commander of the Data Systems unit of The White House Communications Agency, one of my many jobs was communications to the bunker. Most of this part of what my unit did is classified, so I will not talk any more about their mission or how they did their mission. But it makes sense that if the President is going to get stuck in a bunker under The White House that he has to have the ability to communicate outside of his bunker. My team made this happen. My team manned locations on The White House grounds and performed their mission twenty-four hours a day, 7 days a week, 365 days a year. I had the best communication people that the service had to offer working for me. My team was in charge of all digital and voice communications. That included the famous communication line between The White House and Moscow. Again, in open source material, there is no real red phone between The White House and Moscow, it is a teletype system. The team of Russian translators and communications specialist worked for me and manned their post twenty-four hours a day. What a great group of dedicated military members.

Like the other areas of The White House the bunker was run by the Military. In this case the Navy ran the bunker complex. They had great knowledge of how to engineer a compartmentalized area, with generator power. It was just like a submarine must be self-sustaining with power, air, water, so did the bunker.

I got to sleep in the bunker about once a week when I was on duty as the Presidential Communications Officer (PCO). Sleeping at The White House, working in and outside of the bunker and other areas of The White House was a great experience and I hope I give you some ideas of what that was like.

CAMP DAVID

Camp David is the most well-known Presidential country retreat. It is located in the wooded hills of Catoctin Mountain Park near Thurmont, Maryland about 62 miles north-northwest of Washington, D.C. It is officially known as the Naval Support Facility Thurmont, because it is technically a military installation, and staffing is primarily provided by the Navy and the Marines.

Camp David was originally built as a camp for federal government agents and their families. Construction started in 1935 and was completed in 1938. In 1942 President Roosevelt converted it to a presidential retreat to provide the President a safe and relaxing residence away from The White House. Navy and Marines personnel are stationed at Camp David year-round and keep this facility up and operating all the time just in case the President wants to comes out.

I had the opportunity to fly out to Camp David several times with the President and his family. I never got a chance to stay there overnight, but I did get to walk the grounds and it was beautiful out there.

THE WHITE HOUSE TRANSPORTATION AGENCY

The White House Transportation Agency (aka White House Garage) was created in 1909 when The White House stables were converted into a garage for The White House's first vehicles. The White House Garage is staffed by Army noncommissioned officer master drivers. The White House Transportation Agency provides a fleet of motor vehicles and transportation services to the First Family, White House staff, and official visitors. This include providing transportation for the Presidential motorcades. The agency's soldiers work closely with the Secret Service both in training and in motorcade support. The Secret Service drives the Presidential Limo and a couple of their support cars in the motorcade, the rest are driven by WHTA soldiers.

WHITE HOUSE AIRLIFT OPERATIONS

President Franklin D. Roosevelt called for the creation of the Presidential Pilot's Office (renamed the Presidential Airlift Group in 2001) to provide air transportation to the President and his staff. This group which is housed in the Old Executive Office Building on the 18 Acres White House compound coordinates all travel operations between The White House and its support airlift agencies.

AIR FORCE ONE

Air Force One is one of the most recognizable symbols of the Presidency. Technically, "Air Force One" is the official air traffic control call sign for any aircraft carrying the President of the United States. The "Air Force One" call sign was created after a 1953 incident during which a Lockheed Constellation named Columbine II, carrying President Dwight D. Eisenhower, entered the same airspace as a commercial airline flight using the same call sign.

A number of aircraft types have been used as Air Force One since the creation of the Presidential fleet. Since 1990, the Presidential fleet has been two almost identical Boeing VC-25As, which are specifically configured, highly customized Boeing 747-200B series aircraft. First Lady Jacqueline Kennedy contracted designer Raymond Loewy who came up with the exterior design. The polished aluminum fuselage on the bottom side and then used two blues on the top with the white. The Presidential Seal were added to both sides along with the US flag on the tail. The tail number (also called tail codes) for these two nearly identical 747's are 28000 and 29000. These numbers are used when designating the aircraft when the President is not on board, Special Air Mission (SAM) 2800 or SAM 2900.

In 1997 while I was at The White House the move "Air Force One," came out in theaters. I was amazed at how accurate they had the main cabin layout compared to the real Air Force One. Of course, there is no gun closet as shown in the movie but the rest of it was pretty much on target on the main floor. The movie totally made up many things about the belly part of the plane, there is no survival pod, or paratrooper door. The movie also had the top communications portion of the plane a little off, there is not enough space to have a fight as shown in the movie in this area. The movie had several things that were not real in it, but after all it was a movie. But it was still amazing that some of the staffers at The White House came to me after they saw that movie and wanted a cellphone like the one in the move. This type of cellphone that could place a call inside an aircraft moving at hundreds of miles an hour, 30 or 40 thousand feet up in the air using simple cellphone technology did not exist in the mid-90s.

Me in front of the steps up to Air Force One

This type of thing happened all the time when staffers saw something in the news, in an advertisement, or in the movies, and they would want whatever it was right away. However, the items they would ask for were made up by the movie people and this type of mobile phone that could be used on a plan did not existed in 1997. I had to explain to The White House staff over and over again every time they heard or saw a new type of technology.

It is very hard to get onto Air Force One. You have to be on the manifest to travel on the aircraft and that is not an easy thing to do. My bosses or his deputy flew on every flight with the President. As one of a few senior Presidential Communications Officer (PCO) my last couple of years we always had to be ready to fly on Air Force One as the White House Communications Agency representative. I was never selected to travel on Air Force One, but I did get several chances to get on board and do a tour of the plane.

On one trip, I was selected for a visit near to my home town of Boca Raton. The visit was to West Palm Beach, Florida. I was able to get my Mom to meet President Clinton and take a photo with him (see Chapter 13). I was also able to get my Mom a tour of Air Force One. You don't get many perks for working at The White House but getting family members a photo with the President and getting your family a tour of Air Force One is one of those things that makes this job special.

MARINE ONE

The Marine Helicopter Squadron One (HMX-1) was created in 1957 when President Dwight D. Eisenhower was vacationing in Newport, Rhode Island and had to return to The White House on short notice. President Eisenhower was the first president to use a helicopter and decided that this mode of transportation was needed.

Since 1976 the Marine Corps was assigned the mission of providing helicopter support to the President. Any Marine helicopter which has the President aboard uses the call sign "Marine One." Today HMX-1 also supports the Vice President, Secretary of Defense, Secretary of the Navy, Commandant of the Marine Corps, and all visiting Heads of States in the Washington, D.C. area. Currently the fleet is made up of the VH-3D Sea Kings and VH-60N Black Hawks. Because of the distinctive design with a white top over a green body the Presidential VH-60N are called White Hawks. The V designates the aircraft as configured for use by VIPs. The VH-3D is capable of transporting fourteen passengers while the VH-60N seats eleven.

I flew on the helicopters all the time. There is a seat for the Communications officer that sits right across from the President. Every time the helicopters is used, a Presidential Communications Officer has to test the communications gear and travels with the helicopter.

Here I am getting ready to board HMX1

On several occasions I flew on the Presidential helicopters to and from the South Lawn when no one else was on the helicopter. When no one else is on the helicopter you can look out the windows and be a tourist, even take some pictures. Flying off of the South lawn of The White House and flying right next to the Washington monument is so cool.

WHITE HOUSE COMMUNICATIONS AGENCY (WHCA)

The White House Communications Agency (WHCA), originally known as The White House Signal Detachment was officially formed by the War Department on 25 March

1942 during World War II, and the Roosevelt Administration. The organization was created to provide normal and emergency communications requirements in support of the President.

The current mission statement for The White House Communications Agency is to, "Provide instantaneous safe & secure communications and five-minute records communications anytime, anywhere, for the President and The White House." WHCA is a military joint organization composed of Army, Air Force, Navy, Marine, and a few Coast Guard personnel. WHCA has played a silent and significant role in many historical events to include WWII, through todays conflicts. WHCA was also a key player in documenting the assassination of President Kennedy and the attempts on the lives of Presidents Ford and Reagan.

I was interviewed and hired to work for WHCA to support the President, not only in my day time job as the Commander of the Data Systems Unit but also to be a Presidential Communication Officer (PCO).

There are thousands of military members from all services supporting the Commander-in-Chief and The White House. I have only touched on a few of the different units, the ones I worked with the most. All these different units had outstanding military members that where the best of the best in their fields. I was so proud and honored to work with these individual's day after day on a real world and important mission!

CHAPTER 4

My Daytime Job at The White House

Over the four and a half years I was at The White House I had several different day time jobs. The job that I enjoyed the most was being the Commander, Data Systems Unit. The civilian equivalent title would be the Chief Information Officer (CIO) of The White House. In this position I supported all the classified Information Technology for the President, the Vice President, and The White House staff.

HEAD/DIRECTOR OF HUMAN RESOURCES

As stated in the beginning of this book I was originally interviewed and hired, to be the Director of the Human Resource team. I was hired to improve the HR division and turn them into one cohesive and outstanding team. The White House Communications Agency was a joint agency, with all services (Army, Air Force, Navy, Marine, and a few Coast Guards) working for it. Even though WHCA had been a multi-service joint agency for quite some time, the HR team had a distinctive Army feel. Many of the senior members on the HR team were Army and they thought like outstanding HR people doing things in an Army way. I saw this as one of the major issues to fix. The HR team needed to support all their military members. They needed outstanding HR members from each service that would deal with each service personnel issues. The current set up lead to a distinctive lack of understanding cross the services. It was not one team, it was a bunch of separate groups trying to get the job done with minimal understanding from the other teams on why things were done one way within one service and why things were done a different way in a different service. This caused a lot of tension and misunderstanding.

I started on my mission to improve the HR team right away. I started working on their issues before I even got to The White House. While I was in Cairo, working out of the embassy for the Bright Star exercise. I would have a conference call at the beginning of my day, which would be the end of the East Coast work day. I would do the same thing at the end of my very long work day in Cairo, which would be the beginning of the next work day on the East Coast. I would bring in the most senior person of each service, that I had working for me, and have them talk about their issues. We did this for several weeks until I understood what was going on. I would talk to each member of the team both in the two a day staff calls and by setting up one on one counseling calls with each individual. A picture was forming for me of the major issues. We had individual all-stars but they we not working as a team. They were not use to working and trusting a team or other team member to have their back.

The first thing I did was to hire a senior non-commissioned officer that was an Air Force Chief Master Sergeant, that I knew. I also hired a Navy Senior Chief to be the number two senior Non-commissioned Officer on my leadership team. I already had my friend the Army Warrant Officer. So now my senior team had all three major services on it. That was a good start. Then I told these three that they would not manage their own service, but they would manage a mixture of service members under them. I broke up the services and moved them into areas that they knew little about and told them to cross train and learn each services regulation, the job and how the job was done for that service.

The first month of doing this the team failed several times and it was noticeable all the way up the chain to the top. I ask that they have faith in me and to let me continue down the road of what I was doing, even though I was not there I knew what was going on. I had already told my new boss that we may have a few problems before things got better so he was ready for our failures. The one thing about type A people that are the best at what they do, they do not like to fail. They will beat themselves up a lot harder than I could do. They worked hard to learn their new jobs to show the new boss that they could do anything. Remember these folks were the best of the best that how they got here. These folks did not disappoint. At the end of three months while I was in Cairo doing all these conference calls I could tell things had improved and we were moving in the right direction. The great individuals were now forming a team, they were depending on not just themselves but they were depending on information that their team members had to get the job done. One person could now go on vacation and things would not stop because others knew the job and could continue doing it. The cross training became a key part of what I did. Every Wednesday afternoon from 1:00 P.M. to 4:00 P.M. I closed the Human Resources department and they did training, and cross training.

By the time I showed up at The White House in January 1995, I had been running the Human Resources department from Cairo for over four months and it was working great. Things were getting done, moral was the highest it had ever been, and no complaints were being made about HR issues.

When I walked in the door at my new unit I had already worked my way out of the job. They didn't need me because the HR leadership team I had put in place was running smoothly just the way they were. As I mentioned in Chapter 2 the Commander of WHCA asked me if I could do this same thing with the Information Technology department. He wanted me to help the IT team improve like I had improved the HR team. He told me that I would have to be the Deputy Commander, the number two person on the Information Technology team. I said, "Yes." I wanted to work in the IT field taking the Deputy job got me there.

DEPUTY COMMANDER, DATA SYSTEM UNIT

After the discussion with the WHCA Commander, I started in my new position as Deputy Commander, Data System Unit on my first day in the door. I understood that I wasn't the top dog, I was the deputy, the number two person in the unit, but that was ok with me. As mentioned in Chapter 2, the person that interviewed and received the Commander position was an Air Force Lieutenant Colonel with great technical skill sets. I was looking forward to see what I could learn from him, especially his technical skills. He had been in Command already for about six months. When I met him and we talked about how we would be a team to run the Data Systems Unit, I could tell he really knew the technical side of Information Technology. I thought I knew a lot about technology but over the next six months I learned a ton more. I enjoyed my day the job, and I also enjoyed my side job of being a President Communications Officer (PCO). I was learning both these jobs at the same time, which was a lot to take in. I now understood why they had both a Commander and a Deputy Commander over the Data Systems Unit. One of us was always traveling or being pulled away from our day job to be a PCO or do another White House duties. With two of us in the Command Section there was always one of us in the office to run the automation for The White House. I didn't realize it at the time I accepted the Deputy position that this was the best decision I could have made. Coming in as the Deputy really helped me out, by giving me time to learn all the things I needed to succeed at The White House.

I was asked to improve the IT team when I took the job, but I found this to be very difficult to accomplish this mission as the Deputy Commander. I tried to make changes to help the Data System Unit function better but, the current Commander had a different management style and my changes were not accepted. He was a much more technical officer and ran the unit in an autocratic style thinking only about technology changes. He did not understand or know his people, as well as I did. He did a great job at start technology improvements at The White House, which were much needed. We started transitioning from the old mainframe computing technology to new client server technology. We improved technology at The White House by providing outstanding new capabilities. You have to remember this was the mid-90s and computers in the office space was still relatively new.

I learned a lot about Information Technology during this time of my like. Much of which I still use today in my civilian Information Technology jobs. I also learned more about leadership. The current Commanders leadership still did not build esprit-de-corps in the unit, it did not help the individual, but it did meet the technology mission that we had. I wanted to make changes, I was hired to make things better, but I could not make that happen. When you are the Deputy, you have to let the Commander lead the unit the way he wants to and you have to support.

One day the Commander of The White House Communications Agency called me into his office and asked me why I had not fixed the Information Technology team like I had with the Human Resources team. I told him what I just told you all. You have to support the Commander in charge on how he wants to do things. If you provided input and he does not take it there is not much you can do about that. You just have to salute, say "Yes sir," and drive on.

I was then told that the current Commander had just came out of the Colonel's list to get promoted and was also picked up to go to the War College, which is the top educational institute in the Military. He would be leaving immediately for school. The Commander then told me he knew this was coming and had to wait until it was officially release before he could tell me. He then told me that he was putting me in charge and now it was time to make the changes I wanted to do, to get that team going just like the HR team. He told me that I was taking Command of the Data Systems Unit and to make it happen.

COMMANDER, DATA SYSTEM UNIT (THE WHITE HOUSE CIO)

I became Command of the Data System Unit in a nice small tasteful Change of Command ceremony that took place on the Data Center floor. This was a top-secret vault area that you had to have a need to know to enter, so my wife and kids were not able to attend. It was a once in a life time opportunity to have this even in an area that no one else could. Since it was a Top-Secret compartmentalized facility no pictures could be taken, so I don't have any pictures of this once in a life time event. But, I do have the memories of this event and that is all that really counts.

I was now in charge of all classified communication and technology support to the President, the Vice President, and The White House Staff. I was in charge of the people that worked in the Situation Room, in the Communications Bunker, of the Moscow hotline, the primary Data Center, and the backup disaster recover Data Centers. This was a hugely stressful job, but this is what I wanted. Now I was doing exactly what I wanted to do. I was not only the Commander of the Data Systems Unit, but I was also the Chief Information Officer (CIO) and the Chief Information Security Officer (CISO) for all classified information technology at The White House.

I now had to go to the National Defense University to be certify as a Government Chief Information Officer (CIO). Over the next year I took courses at the National Defense University in D.C. to be one of the first 100 certified CIOs for the Government. There was a new law that stated any head of a major government agency had to be trained and certified for this new area of IT and the new title of CIO. I learned a lot about being a Chief Information Officer, the political side of the job, along with the budget side.

I continued the Data Centers transition from the old big blue IBM main frame data center computers. These were reel to reel tape type machines to the new, just on the market, client server Data Center technology. Before I left the CIO job, I had transitioned all our primary and back up Data Centers to client server technology. We went from a computer room floor that was the size of a football field to two or three racks of servers that could have fit into a small bedroom size space. We had so much extra room in the Data Center that I move cubicles and people into the left-over space and consolidated several sections into one area. This increased communications and coordination between these teams. Greatly improved productivity of this section.

Do you remember Y2K (year 2000)? It was the transitioning of the calendar from the 1900 century to the 2000 century. This really was the discovery that not all computers could handle the date change from two digits to four. This was a big thing for the computer field. I took Command of the Data System Units in 1995 and Y2K was on our mind already. The White House wanted to make sure that everything would work on 1 January 2000. We started our transition planning in 1995 to make sure there were no issues with any of our systems and our software. The White House was way head of the game, we started five years early. We were transitioning our software and hardware to new equipment that was ready for the change of the centuries to 2000. We were transitioning everything from our email system which was LOTUS notes to a new updated email system.

Another big area of responsibility for me was maintaining historical Presidential records. The old data from previous Presidents that were in our old computer systems that we were replacing. This whole Y2K issue that brought about the upgrading of computer systems within the government brought up a lot of discussion between several government agencies and the National Archives about what to do with old data. We had to retain the old data and still had to have the ability to move to new technology. The Government and this case the National Archives, needed to come up with a set of standards that would allow for storable and searchable data that would not be affected by the changes in technology. As the individual responsible for all the classified Presidential records I had a big say in how we were going to handle old data. All the data I had must be kept as historical Presidential activities. Even though most of my data was classified today, almost all classified documents can and will be declassified with the passage of time. Eventually 95% of classified material will be declassified in 25 or 50 years. We had to make sure that the material I had for both President Clinton and for the previous presidents, could be used later on in history.

I sat on a panel of government CIOs and we worked with the National Archives and the library of congress to come up with the American Standard Code for Information Interchange (or as it is better known ASCII) as the basic storage technology to use. After that decision was made, we started to transfer all the historical Presidential data into the new storage standards for the history of our country. I still had reels and reels of the Nixon tapes in my data center and they all needed to be transferred into long term storage standards. I had a full time IBM contract team working just on the Nixon tapes and all that data into long term searchable storage. Before I left The White House, all of the old Nixon tapes and old Presidential data had been transitioned into the new long-term storage standards and handed over to the National Archives.

I think Chaucer said "All good things must come to an end." I loved being the Commander over the Data Systems Unit. I was the leader of an outstanding unit of great men and women that had one of the most important jobs in the government. My team managing all the classified Information Technology that came into and went out of The White House. What we did every day mattered to this country and to the world. The President could not have accomplished his job without my teams support and everyone on my team knew this! I was leading over 300 people, working on a mission that was important and demanding. I had the best of the best the military had to offer working under my Command. Who would not love this job! I loved this job!

This was a once in a life time opportunity and I was having the time of my life. But all good things come to an end and so it was for this position, being the Commander of the Data Systems Unit at The White House Communications Agency. My boss, the Commander, of The White House Communications Agency decided to reorganize the agency and take away all the Command positions under him. He turned all the Command positions into staff positions. In losing the Command title and position you also lose most of the ability to directly affect the military members working under you. I could take liberties as a commander to support my troops, with time off, with awards, with liberal or harsh punishment when needed. You get to know your troops, their problems, their families, and you are a real team in a command structure organization. I did as I was told and closed down the Command of Data Systems Unit and turn it into a staff organization.

I had finished over two and a half years at The White House as first the Deputy Commander and then the Commander of the Data Systems Unit. I was sad to see that Command get shut down and it being turned into a staff position. But it was good timing for me, it was time for me to move to a new unit and job. Joint jobs are usually only two years long and I had already been at The White House for two and a half years. I had fixed the HR team and I had fixed the IT team, what was next for me. I was ready to move, I was looking forwards to a new challenge at a new unit and to find things I could fix.

However, the new Commander of The White House Communications Agency who had just taken over had heard about all I had done with the HR team and IT team. He personally asked me to stay on for a second tour at The White House. I gave his request some thought, keeping my family in one place and not having to move was a plus. Staying in an organization that made a difference at the highest levels of the Government, working with outstanding military members of all branches was another big plus. Of course, I said "Yes," I would stay for two more years!

DIRECTOR OF TRAINING

I was asked to stay on as the Director of the Training Department of the White House Communications Agency. I had come to this organization as an outsider with outsider ideas and knowledge. Now they were asking me to train people in all forms of Communications. I was not a Signal

Officer and did not have communications as a primary background. I was a Human Resource and an Information Technology person. But, I did know people, what made them tick, what they needed to be happy and what to give them to get the most out of them in their jobs. I also knew systems and how to develop policies and procedures to align the people the process. I knew how to pick things apart to the lowest levels and then rebuild them so they would work efficiently. This is why they asked me to stay and run the Training Department.

The mission of The White House Communications Agency was; Communications in all forms, voice and data. We all had our primary jobs, our day jobs, but we all had secondary jobs too. As I mentioned previously my second job was being a Presidential Communications Officer (PCO). When I started as a PCO I did not know communications at the same level as my peers. So, I kept asking questions, making cheat sheets, writing things down so that they made sense to the average person.

WHCA had a lot of different people doing a lot of things outside of their knowledge base, just like me. These people had to get trained on all types of equipment across. What they needed is cheat sheets that the average person could understand and I knew how to do that.

Remember we had the best of all the services working here. These where people that could pick up knowledge very well, if provided the right materials and training. So, that is what I did for my next two years at The White House. I helped train a vehicle mechanic how to set up a satellite dish. I helped train a radio operator how to run a full audio visional set up for the President. Everyone had to learn everyone else's job, you never knew what was going to happen and every one had to be ready for everything.

I enjoyed learning and teaching others, much more than I thought I would. I was also able to travel a lot more with the President now that my day job was in training. I was more available during the day in this particular day job then I was when I was in charge of all the Information Technology. By this time, I was one of the most senior officers within The White House Communications Agency. I was handpicked for many of the most difficult assignments overseas. I was selected to manage two of President Clinton's most important trips, one to Beijing, China and the other to Moscow, Russia. Read about these trips in a later chapter.

The next chapter will talk about my job as a Presidential Communication Officer (PCO) and traveling with the President around the world, hearing and seeing things that most people would not believe.

CHAPTER 5

The Presidential Communications Officer Job

Being a Presidential Communications Officer (PCO) was the most important job I will ever have in my life. I was responsible for the last link of communications between the President of the United States and the rest of the world. What a stressful and rewarding job, supporting our nation and knowing that what I did every day made a difference.

THE FOUR HORSEMEN – ALWAYS WITH THE POTUS!

I learned very quickly that there were four positions that were always with the President of The United States (POTUS). I do mean physically next to, around, and within a safe distance of the President twenty-four hours a day, seven days a week, 365 days a year. The four positions where off handily called the "Four Horsemen" from the last book of the New Testament of the Bible "The Four Horsemen of the Apocalypse" that signified Conquest, War, Famine, and Death.

The four positions with the President at all times, where the "SAC", the "Doc", the "MilAide", and the "PCO." These four positions where filled with a rotation of very qualified personnel. These four positions would be in the motorcade, on the helicopters, in AF1, and even stayed in The White

House overnight. Because of these four positions the President could do his job no matter where he was and what was happening in the world.

The "SAC" or Senior Agent in Charge (SAC) position was filled by the Senior Secret Service Agent on the Presidential detail. This position was responsible for the protection of the President. He was responsible for the inner bubble of protection and to make sure all the contingency plans were made just in case one of the outer bubbles of protect got breached. The SAC had final say on security, and his say would override everyone else's, even the Presidents.

The "Doc" or Senior medical person on the daily detail. The Doc position was sometimes held by the actual White House Medical Doctor on staff, like the President's personal physician. While I was at The White House Dr. (Rear Admiral) Connie Mariano held the position of personal physician to the President. The White House Medical Unit had many other medical personnel to include other Doctors, Physician's Assistants, and Emergency Room Trauma Nurses. Any one of these White House Medical Unit personnel would hold down the medical position ready to support the President.

The "MilAide" or Military Aide to the President of the United States. There are five Military Aides to the President, one for each service (Army, Navy, Air Force, Marines, and Coast Guard). One of them is always within a close distance of the President caring the satchel. Most people call the satchel carried by the MilAide the "Nuclear Football." The satchel which is more like a small suitcase contains all the top security information the President may need during an emergency. The top-secret book of plans with multiple options for any different type of event that the President may have to take action on. The president could just pick from an already thought through set of options; if A happens then you can do B, C, or D. These plans are always updated with current. The MilAide would also have all the classified communications codes and code words in the football.

The MilAide carried lot of other things in that satchel. It was like carrying a large bag of goodies for the President. If the President needed something the MilAide would carry it. There where little Presidential gifts, like Presidential tie tacks, or cufflinks or other little items if the President wanted to hand a gift to someone. Sometimes the MilAide would carry around snacks and a soda for the President. The list of things that the MilAide carried for the President was never ending.

The "PCO" or Presidential Communications Officer (PCO) was the fourth positions. I learned very quickly that I was going to be a PCO and would have to learn this job and be one of the "Four Horseman." The PCO had the communications capability to reach back to the rest of the nation and the world. It does do much good for the MilAide to have all these Top-Secret plans, if the President cannot communicate that decisions to the right agencies. The PCO's job was to have multiple ways to communicate back to the government, to the Pentagon, to the State Department, to the Congress, to whoever the President wanted to talk to. We were the telephone guys always making sure that if the President wanted to make a call he could. Whether on a golf course, on a boat in the Mediterranean, or horseback riding in the middle of Argentina he could turn around at a moment's notice and tell the PCO that he wanted to contact anyone in the world and we made that happen.

The President on one of his many golf outings

Being one of the four horsemen in very close proximity to the President gave me the ability to observe a lot about the Clinton White House. I may have only been a communications or telephone guy, but I got to sit in on a lot of meetings against the wall making sure that if the President needed to reach out to someone he could. Being a fly on the wall lead to some unique revelations about the Clinton White House and about how politics and the media work.

THE PCO EQUIPMENT

The first piece of equipment I was given as a Presidential Communications Officer (PCO) was my White House flip badge. I would use this badge many times during my career at The White House. The badge had my newly taken picture on it, had a picture of The White House on it and had verbiage that stated that the individual with the badge was working in direct support of the President of the United States. When people saw this badge, it opened a lot of doors with little to no questions. I was told when I received the badge that I had to keep it with me all time, never to leave it behind when I left the house. When I left The White House, I was given the honor of being able to keep my badge. The badge was voided across the front and mounted onto a wall plaque. I still have my badge proudly displayed on the wall in my home office.

The second piece of equipment I was given, was a White House Communications Agency (WHCA) pin. The WHCA pins were used during official Presidential events. Each agency had their own pins. These pins were all very accountable. This was a quick way to identify who each person was and what their responsibility was. They still use the pin system today to identify which individuals have which access and what they do. All the WHCA pins are numbered and are kept under close accountability. The color and the symbols and the design of the pins change over time. You turn in your old pin and get the new pin on a recurring basis. You are supposed to keep the pin with you at all time just like your White House badge. If you lose a pin or a badge, everything stops, everyone starts looking for the badge or pin until it is found. If the pin is not found everyone in the agency has to change out their pin for a new pin. This is costly and time consuming and whoever loses their pin is greatly chastised by everyone in multiple organizations. No one ever wants to lose a pin or a badge, the peer pressure is overbearing. You might as well leave The White House job when this happens.

The third piece of equipment that you are assigned is your White House Radio (with encryption) and your earplug/mic cable. This radio is another thing you are supposed to keep with you at all time. The encryption within the radio is changed on a recurring basis. You have to bring in your radio on a recurring basis to get the new encryptions codes installed into them. These radios are used when you are on duty to talk to the U.S. Secret Service and back to the Communications Operations Center.

These items that are assigned to you, you had to keep with you when on duty, when at home, and when you are on vacation. You never knew when you were going to get a call to support the needs of the President. I received several calls to come and support, while I was at work, at home, and on vacations. I had a lockable brief case that I kept with me that had White House equipment in it. I always ready, that was the job.

LEARNING THE PCO JOB

When I started as a Presidential Communications Officer (PCO), there was so much to learn, I had no idea how I was ever going to learn it all. The Army trained me to be an outstanding at Human Resource and Information Technology leader. Now I had to learn all the skills it would take to be a PCO. The majority of skills I needed as a PCO were in the very large field of communications. I also needed to learn all sorts of other technology like Audio Video, Lighting, and Teleprompters. I needed to pick up these new skills fast and be 100% perfect in using the tools. This was a very big stretch for me, but I was up to the challenge, I thrived on learning new things. Plus, I already had some communications skills and background. Not as much as I needed for this job, but a least I was not starting from scratch. The real saver for me was the outstanding military members working at The White House, that could help me, train me, teach me, and cover by back side. If I ever had a question or needed help I knew one of them would have the answer or could help me.

As I stated earlier in the book, the mission of the White House Communications Agency was to "Provide instantaneous safe & secure communications and five-minute records communications anytime, anywhere, for the President and The White House." The key to meeting this mission was the PCO. That position was always with the President and was the last link of that chain to make this mission happen. As a side note, the White House Communications Agency was also in charge of the historical records of the President. Recording whatever was said for the National Archives of the United States. This meant we also did a lot of Audio Visual (AV) work with podiums, lights, speakers, and recordings. Where I had some background in communications, I had no background at all in AV. I felt totally lost in this area and if it was not for the outstanding military members that worked in this area I would have been totally lost.

I started my training as a PCO by going to the WHCA warehouse, where all the travel equipment was kept. This was a hugh warehouse with fork lifts and stacks and stacks of communications equipment, telephone switching equipment, satellite equipment, microwave relay equipment, portable cellphone towers, rolls of telephone wire, High Frequency/Ultra High Frequency/Very High Frequency (HF/UHF/VHF) radio equipment, podiums, lights, speakers, and much more. I worked packing and unpacking equipment. At testing the equipment to ensure it was ready for use and more.

When you check equipment, you have known what you are checking, why you are checking it, and how to trouble shoot any problems. This is a great way to learn all about the equipment. We had equipment packing list for each box that help make sure I put the right things in the right box. We also did security checks on the equipment to make sure it was not tampered with during the last trip. I did this type of work for about a week. I was shadowing outstanding military folks that knew what they were doing and helping them with my education and training. It made no difference to anyone in the warehouse what my rank was. We were all there to do a job and the fact that I was a Lieutenant Colonel in the Army didn't matter. I was still one of the team and had to learn the same things that the troops below me had to learn. This was both humbling at the amount of knowledge I had to learn and team building at the same time. The troops saw me in the warehouse rolling up my sleeves right beside them and I earned their respect for how quickly I learned and was able to understand the work load of the enlisted members doing these jobs. Not to mention, I was also doing the job alongside of them, teamwork!

PRESIDENTIAL PODIUM (LECTERN)

One of the areas I trained in was the fabrication shop. I was unaware that our agency built the Presidential Podiums for every President and Vice President. Ok, they were really lecterns, podiums you stand on and lecterns you stand behind, however, everyone at The White House called these items the Presidential Podium. I had not really given it much thought but every President is a different height. Some Presidents are short and some are tall and the podium had to fit that size of President. When a new President is elected, we get their height and build Presidential Podiums to fit that President. President Clinton was six feet and two inches. Because of the height of President Clinton at over six feet and the podium was built for him, some shorter heads of state could barely see over the podium. We fixed this issue by building in a pull-out step into the bottom of the podium. You could hook the toe of your foot into the step and pull it out without anyone really noticing and then stand behind the podium on the step and be high enough to look over the microphones.

We would transport these podiums (along with a lot of other equipment) to every event that the President spoke at. We had big shipping containers that these podiums fit into. As would be expected these podiums were very heavy, no wind was going to blow these over, plus one may want to think about who was standing behind these podiums; they may have had more inside of them then the normal run of the mill podium I would imagine.

The President Podium with Seal – my team setting it up

The podium had special non-reflective paint on the top area for the lighting used. We had to make sure we informed every person that used the podium not to put their hands up on the right and left side of the podium on top of the special paint. Hands had natural oils that would be absorbed by this paint and would leave hand prints on the podium. Of course, people never listen to what you tell them so we had to carry touch up paint with us and fix the podiums over and over again.

Another thing about the podium was the Presidential Seal that goes on the front. Most of the time WHCA set up the podium for an event a day or two before it was used. This allowed for the ability to do sound checks with the microphones on the podium and testing the lighting. Sometimes, the Presidential Podium would be used by others during an event. On these occasions the Presidential Seal would not be on the podium. The seal was only put on the podium when the President entered the building of the event. One of the PCO's job was to walk out on stage and hang the Presidential Seal on the podium when it was time. I had the honor of doing this many, many times during my years at The White House. It was funny how the atmosphere in the room, the noise in the room, would all change when they saw the seal on the podium. Everyone in the room would settle down and get ready for the Presidential announce, of his arrival into the room/stage.

Another unique thing about the Presidential podium was that microphones on it belonged to and the government. There were only two microphones on the podium a primary and a backup. The White House Communications Agency personnel would set up the podium and the microphones and run them through a WHCA sound board and then provide the live feeds to the press. All the press would get the exact same feed at the exact same time. Anything the President said was official public record and had to be recorded and provided to the National Archives. WHCA had the responsibility to record the feed and keep the Presidential Record of what went over the microphones.

THE WHITE HOUSE PRESS POOL

Anyone that has watched the news has seen The White House Press Office gives Presidential press briefings in The White House Press Pool area. This area is a lot smaller than it looks on TV. The podium and its microphones are part of what the White House Communications Agency is responsible for. Again, anything said by The White House becomes public record and has to be stored and provided to the National Archives. That is the job of WHCA. During the normal duty day WHCA has an Audio-Visual Technician onsite at The White House to turn on and run the microphones in the Press Pool area. During the non-work hours, the Presidential Communications Officer (PCO) is responsible to run the Press Pool Audio Visional (A/V) equipment.

In today's world events happen twenty-four hours a day, seven days a week and The White House could at any time call a press conference so WHCA had to have someone on the 18 Acres able to run the equipment needed. Some of the times that was me, when I was pulling PCO duty. This was one of the scariest thing I had to do, because I was not proficient in the A/V equipment. I did not work with this equipment enough to have confidence in my ability. Most of the time I had a technician helping me when I did AV stuff. But in case of an emergency it would have been on my shoulders to make it happen. I just hoped that when I was on duty nothing would come up that would make The White House call an impromptu press conference.

Me at the Podium in the Press Pool Briefing Room

I would go into the Press Pool room every time I went on shift as a PCO and would review the quick reference guide that was laminated and attached to the A/V equipment. This quick reference guide was made specifically for the PCOs that did not do work this equipment every day. I would show step by step instructions to get the system up and running quickly. The AV station also had a large binder with all the trouble shooting guides if something didn't work correctly. But that binder was so big you would be hard pressed to find the one thing you needed to fix something.

The A/V station in The White House Press Pool area was to the right of the podium that you see on TV. Think of a small old-style telephone booth crammed from ceiling to floor with A/V equipment. The A/V station was so tight in space there was not even a chair to sit down on but a stand-up stool to lean against. We had a blue curtain covering our A/V space, just like the blue curtain behind the podium. You felt like you were in a coffin when you went behind the blue curtain to run the A/V equipment.

During my time at The White House I was called upon a couple of times to get the Press Room set up for an off-hour press conferences. Luckily however I never had to run the A/V equipment during the actual press conference. We had an on-call list of A/V Technicians that we would call as soon as The White House ask for an off-hour press conferences. It was the PCO's job to get the Press Room ready and turned on and test all the equipment. We also coordinated with the TVs and Radio people to help with testing their microphone feeds before the actual conference. Most of scheduled press conferences, you were given at least an hour to get ready. Even though some radio and TV stations kept people on The White House grounds from early morning to very late at night not all the pool teams did. The White House usually had to give notice to the full press pool that a conference was going to happen. So normally for these emergency off hours press conferences there was at least an hour notice.

ROAD RUNNER

The White House Communications Agency had multiple communications vehicles that we called "Road Runners." I spent a week in the motor pool area learning these vehicles and their capabilities. These were highly classified mobile communications platforms. When I was at the White House Communications Agency (WHCA), the Road Runner vehicles were black Ford Econoline vans that were very modified with a full set of mobile communications equipment in the back on racks. This vehicle had its own generator that could run when the vehicle was turned off. It also had connections on the outside of the vehicle where we could plug it into building power and plug it into normal telephone lines. This vehicle was amazing in all that it could do in a small mobile package. We had mobile satellite communications that worked very well even when the vehicle was moving 55 miles an hour. You have to remember this was back in the mid-90s before cellphones systems had really taken off and before all the different types of satellite system we have today. This vehicle was way ahead of its time.

We had a motor pool full of these vehicles maybe around twenty. We would fly them on US Air Force cargo planes to every stop the President would go to. These vehicles were always in the motorcade and provided mobile communications within the motorcade. It was like moving a mobile switch board with you everywhere. We would be able to connect anywhere in the world from that vehicle, using multiple encrypted paths of communications.

The windows on the vehicle were all blacked out and there was a curtain that separated the driver and the back. There were two captain chairs in the back. This vehicle would be manned twenty-four hours a day when it was being used. Some locations we went to did not have good land line capabilities and the Road Runners communications was the only thing we had. The only thing this vehicle didn't have was a bathroom.

Road Runner – Mobile Communications Platform

The Road Runner vehicles that I worked with were top-secret pieces of equipment. However, in my research for this book I have found in open source that the Vans have been replaced with newer black Suburban type vehicles. These new Road Runners I am sure have a full new suite of communications equipment and are much more advanced then the ones I worked with.

REDUNDENT COMMUNICATIONS

To meet the mission of the White House Communications Agency of instantaneous communications we always had multiple and redundant communications channels. This was not that hard to do when we were on The White House grounds, or on any of the aircraft (AF1 or HMX1). In those locations we had all the equipment in place, it was tested and used it on a recurring basis. But when the President left The White House grounds, we would always have to set up multiple redundant communications anywhere he went. This is why the Presidential Communications Officer was always with the President as one of the four horsemen, to provide that communications link back to the rest of the government. We had specialized vehicles like the Road Runner to help during these times, not only within the motorcade when it was moving but also at event locations that it would be parked outside. But these vehicles were not enough. To meet the mission of truly redundant communications, we always had three to five different ways to communicate everywhere we went.

We used these new items called cellphones – we called them BMUS phones. I don't think anyone on The White House Staff knew why we called them BMUS phones. BMUS stood for "Beam Me Up Scotty (BMUS)," because these were flip type phones that look just like the communicators used on Star Trek. The acronym we used was an inside joke for the WHCA folks. We would hand out cellphones to the primary White House staff and the primary Secret Service personnel for each event or trip. We would create phone rosters and pre-program the phones for each event or trip. You never knew what phone number you may end up with until you showed up. I look back at the amount of time and how we did things back in the 90s and think wow things must be so much easier today. We did a lot of work on each and every event just to meet our communications mission. But that was our job!

We used our own White House cellphones, remember this was the mid-90's and there were not as many cellphone towers as there are today. Plus, the civilian system was not secure enough. So, we would set up our own portable cellphone towers along all the motorcade routes, in the areas of the backup routes, emergency landing zones and the event sites. We would tie these mobile cellphone towners into landlines and run it all back to our own telecommunication central hub that we would set up.

We would travel with a portal AT&T communication switch like the phone company uses in small-towns. But ours was a portable switch that we designed and developed to meet The White House needs. How the switch worked was classified back in the 90s, but today's technology has far surpassed what we had.

When we traveled we would take over the whole floor or multiple floors of a hotel. We would have them take the beds out of some of the rooms and put tables and chairs in those rooms. Taking over a full floor of a hotel gave us better security, with sleeping rooms on the ends of the floor and the communications and office rooms in the middle of the floor. We would set up our portable telecommunications switch in one of our communication rooms. That would always have an adjoining room for personnel to hot bunk in. Someone would always be manning the telephone switch and there would always be a backup person sleeping right next door that could be called if an emergency happened.

We would come into a town and have the local telephone company run hard telephone lines to where our office spaces were in a hotel. Sometimes the telephone company would just run a single 100 pair or 250 pair telephone line from the telephone poll outside the hotel straight into the window of the hotel room to get us the phone lines to us in a fast manner.

We not only used hard lines provided by the telephone company at the hotel, we would set up hard lines at each of the event locations for the President. We would put Secure Telephone Units third generation (STUIII) on the end of the civilian telephone lines. These phones used encryptions keys to encrypt right at the telephone unit and those encryption keys would be synced with the switch, or one of our setups at the other end and we could unencrypt or send the voice on encrypted to another STUIII unit or do all sorts of fancy communications switching. This allowed the president and his staff to make both classified and unclassified calls.

Installing a satellite dish on a roof during a trip

We also traveled with portable satellite dishes and portable microwave relay towers. These portable satellite dishes in the mid-90s were not the ones we have today on the side of people's houses that are small and light weight. Oh no the ones in the mid-90 were full twelve-foot round satellite dishes that came in parts that had to be assembled. We would have to carry this equipment up to the roofs of hotels and office buildings to set the equipment up. We used the microwave and satellite dishes a lot more during our overseas trips where we could not count on the civilian telephone lines as much. We always wanted to make sure our host country could not cut us off from communicating.

Lastly, we used HF, VHF, and UHF radios that were encrypted. This was a ton of equipment to travel around the world with and set up. But everywhere the president went we were going to make sure he could communicate with the people he needed to talk to anytime, anywhere

TELEPROMPTER SUPPORT

The White House Communications Agency (WHCA) is also responsible for running the teleprompter support for the President. We maintained the teleprompter, set it up, and run the equipment. This is seen to be part of the official record of the President. Just like WHCA records all speeches and provides that information to the National Archives as part of the official Presidential records. WHCA also provide support in the area of the teleprompter and the records maintain in this area.

The teleprompter is not as fancy as one may think. It is just a computer that uses a teleprompter program that allows the operator to scroll up or down a speech. What shows on the computer screen shows through the cameras that reflect on the glass plates to the right or left of the main podium view. The projector projects the words on the glass at an angle so the audience cannot see the words but the person standing behind the podium can see the refection of the words and can read them.

Usually a paper copy of the speech is provided so that the teleprompter operator can follow along with the speech. This also makes it easier when the President goes off script and jumped around in the speech the teleprompter operator can move/scroll to the new section that the President would be talking about. The President would get accustom to the ability of a specific teleprompter operator, how fast or slow they scrolled. How that operator would be able to fine were the President jumped to in a speech and get the teleprompter back on the script. It took practice and real skill to be an operator. If you were good and the President like the way you did your job you would get stuck into doing teleprompter duty for a long time, over and over again.

The State of the Union and swearing in ceremonies were the most important teleprompter missions. The President and his staff would practice these speeches over and over again and change things over and over again and the teleprompter operator had to get very familiar with the speech so that when the President went off script the teleprompter operator could find the place where the President went to in the speech and catch back up. The teleprompter room/space had a television feed so the teleprompter or his assistant could watch the President in real time. This location also had a direct microphone feed to that room too so they did not have to rely on the TV feed to know what was being said.

This was a very stressful job and people would get fired on the spot for messing up the teleprompter operations. I never had the opportunity to work the teleprompter and I never wanted to.

MOTORCADE

The motorcade is one of the primary means for the President to get from point A to point B. Therefore, taking care of the Presidential communications for a motorcade is a recurring activity for the PCO to take care of.

We had to learn how to open the doors to the limo's which all have special lock. Then, we would get in and sit in the back of the limo in the Presidents seat. We would make test calls with both the phone and the radio in the limo. We would first call the presidential switch board on a civilian line to the non-operational number and tell them that we would be testing the Presidential line. Then we would call using the Presidential line.

Me on the South Lawn in front of the Presidential Limo

The Presidential lines are all indicated at the switch board and they know when one of those lines ring that most likely the President calling. These Presidential lines are covered twenty-four hours a day, seven days a week, 365 days a year, by very highly trained telephone operators with an assistant operator in support. The President picks up the phone and it automatically rings to the switch board. The President tells them who he wants to talk to and then the WHCA switchboard finds that person and puts through that call.

Motorcade lining up on the South Lawn

When you get new guys on the switch board or new PCOs that are in training it is common to mess with them by not telling them to do the pre-heads up call to the switch board. If you don't do the heads up call the switch board treats that call as if you were the President. There is a level of stress that goes with supporting the President that is not needed when it is just a test. The new PCO's would get yelled at by the switch board leader when he hears that the new PCO didn't do a heads up call first. At the same time, it is good training for the switch board always to be ready, when there is a new switch board person on his first shift on the POTUS line, everyone would mess with them. You would call in and they think it's their first Presidential call and you would order a pizza or something. This was a great way to reduce stress in a very stressful job.

All the motorcades in the D.C. area have vehicles provided by The White House Garage and the US Secret Service. These vehicles all have their communication package already in the car with a driver and shot gun person knowing how to use this equipment and doing the test of the equipment. This means a motorcade within D.C. can be done very quickly. Everyone knows what to do and how to do it.

However, the motorcades outside of the D.C. area are accomplished much differently. You still have the limo's and the Secret Service cars that are brought to each event site (via military aircraft in most cases). But almost all the other vehicles are rental cars or vans, driven by volunteer drivers. All these rental vehicles have to be set up with White House radios. The volunteer drivers are not supposed to touch or use the radios, they are for White House use only. Unlike the D.C. motorcades where the driver takes care of the vehicles and the radio checks. When we are on the road the WHCA team has to install the radios and do all the radios checks for all the vehicles. This can take some time.

All the rental vehicles for the motorcade come out to the airport several hours before the motorcade is needed. The first thing that is done is the Secret Service does their security checks on the vehicles. We would do our communications security checks of the vehicles, then we temporarily install White House radios with magnetic antennas mount. It was WHCA responsibility to make sure that all communications for the whole motorcade was up and running by the time the motorcade was needed. The PCO in charge of the airport arrival was overall responsible to make sure WHCA personnel meet this mission.

At the end of the event, when the motorcade is no longer needed. The WHCA personnel would have to pick up all the radios from all the vehicles before they leave. The close out of a motorcade can get very hectic because it is usually at the end of a long day or long trip at a location. The Secret Service would always want to wait until AF1 takes off before releasing the motorcade. You never know what was going to happen so you had to prepared if AF1 returned to the airport. But all the volunteer drivers want to leave right away. It gets to be a real game as to when to pull the equipment so you don't lose anything, by the volunteers driving away with the equipment in the car. The radio equipment was considered very sensitive since they all were encrypted with special White House level encryption. We could not afford to lose any of this sensitive radio equipment. Every time I was the Airport PCO I never had any volunteers drive off with White House radio equipment. I did have to go running down the tarmac after a couple of vehicles once. This was not the same for all the PCO's that did the Airport duty. Several times WHCA would have to track down the volunteer and the rental car and retrieve our equipment after the fact. But you learn over time what to say to the volunteer drivers to put the fear of the Government into them if they take off without being cleared by the PCO.

A standard motorcade is about thirteen cars, some motorcades in foreign countries can get up to twenty-eight cars. Then you add all the police escort cars and motorcycles and it can really get long. The standard motorcade usually has two limos. This allows the limos to constantly switch places as part of operational security so no one knows which limo the president is actually in.

The Road Runner vehicle, that WHCA has in the motorcade to provide communications support, is always in the back of the motorcade with the ambulance. This gives the Road Runner and the ambulance the greatest flexibility to change routes and be the most useful in case of an emergency.

One of the things I found to be the weirdest thing of all, was the press vehicle that was in the motorcade. The press vehicle was towards the end of the motorcade and in front of the Road Runner which is what I traveled in most of the time. This vehicle was for the press that travels with the President on AF1. They get off the back of AF1, down the back stairway and run to the motorcade and get ready for departure. That is normal, the staff does the same thing, run to their cars from AF1. When the President wants to go the motorcades leaves and it will leave without you if you're not already in your car. No one stops the motorcade for anything other than the President himself.

The thing with the press vehicle, however, was there was always someone standing up out of the Sun Roof of the car or van with a video camera taping the motorcade. It didn't make a different if it was cold, raining, snowing, or blistering hot. There was always one cameraman in the press vehicle video recording the motorcade. We called this the press death watch. The press did not want to miss any attack on the motorcade or shooting of the president like with President Kennedy. I understand the reason for the press wanting that video shot if something happened. But I still found it very morbid that on every single motorcade one press guy would videoing the motorcade to get that one shot that would make that person famous.

These motorcades always have a lot of police support, local, state, sheriffs, and motorcycles. Most every type of cop you can think of. Usually at the end of the motorcade, all the motorcycle cops and patrol cops that are at the airport that were in the motorcade quickly (I mean very quickly) get out of their cars and bikes and run up to the bottom of the stairs of AF1. The President usually will take a group photo with all the cops as a thank you for your help.

IN-TOWN EVENTS

Any event that the President went to within the great D.C. area, were considered "in town events. The President went to all type of in town events, like conference, speaking engagements, or just to go get a burger. The President would talk a motorcade to these close in-town events. These in-town events were a great place for a new Presidential Communications Officer (PCO) to start their learning process. The PCO was given the easy tasks for these events as part of our training. After you learned how to set up the motorcade on the south lawn of The White House, your next step would be to learn how to handle calling arrival of the motorcade at an in-town event.

As a side note, I found it funny that the President went to all these fancy five-star hotels, but we always arrived in the back-loading dock area next to were the trash cans would normally be. For security reasons, the big trash dumpsters were all moved out of the loading dock area. But still the

President almost never saw the lobby of all these five-star hotels just the back entrance.

The PCO would stand in the back-loading dock area of a hotel and call over the radio the arrival of the President at the event site. Most of the time, when the President arrives at an event site, the limo is pulled into a secure loading dock area. Because of this, everyone in the motorcade loses site of the limo and the President. It is the PCO's responsibility to keep everyone aware of the Presidents location and actions. The PCO waits for the President inside the loading dock area and calls over the radio something likes "Eagle arrived ABC Hotel loading dock area." President Clinton's call sign was "Eagle." By hearing the Presidents location over the radio, everyone would know exactly where he is. This allows the rest of the people in the motorcade to exit the motorcade and head into the event site. Those motorcade people usually use a special entrance just for them. There is no need for those people to go to the front of the venue and go through magnetometers, since they are all considered cleared already.

When there was not a loading dock to pull the limo into the Secret Service would setup tents. It did not make a difference where, in the middle of roads or in an open field or wherever the Presidential limo stopped. This would block the President from view when he was gets out of the limo. He then walks through a tent walk way into the event location. The reason for this is security, if the bad guys can't see the President, they can't shoot at him. The Secret Service would use all sorts of things like tents, busses, or trucks to block the line of sight view from the bad guys.

There was good reason for the Secret Service use of visual blocking security measures. If you think back to what happened to President Regan at the Washington Hilton hotel. The President was leaving the side doors of the hotel waking to his limo, when he was attacked and shot. The Washington Hilton has since built a garage, in the same location that President Regan was shot. Now the President's limo can pull into an enclosed garage to use the side door of the Washington Hilton. I have worked several events at the Washington Hilton and have walked the same ground as President Regan within the new garage and there is a big security difference today.

What was good for security however was not good for situational awareness for the security teams and for The White House staff. That was why there was always a PCO with the President to communicate over the radio the Presidents locations and his actions of what would be next. The PCO and his team had several other tasks to accomplish at an in-town event. The WHCA team also sets up hold rooms with full White House communications for the Presidents and The White House staff. You never know when the President or staff needs to make a phone call to run the country. We setup a hold rooms at almost every event locations. We also setup the Secret Service command post for all these events. All these locations had Top Secret communications ability.

Continuing, the WHCA personnel were responsible for the official Presidential Podium (like I mentioned before it was really a lectern – but everyone called it the Presidential Podium). The Presidential Podium was setup for all Presidential events. At times the President would not be the only one using the podium. During events many people may be speaking before or after the President. It didn't make sense to stop a conference in the middle and put out a new podium and do all the sound checks. WHCA would setup the podium at the beginning of the day and all the speakers would use the Presidential Podium for that event. The only difference is the Presidential seal would not be on the podium. The seal would only be hung on the podium when the President entered the building or was about to speak. One of the responsibilities of the PCO was to hang the seal on the podium at the right time.

One of the things that happens every now and then is the Seal will fall off the podium at the absolute wrong time. The PCO has to make very sure when he hangs the seal that it is on correctly and will not fall off. The last thing you want to do is crawl out on stage when the President is speaking and re-hang the seal on the podium. Luckily the seal never fell off when I put it on. I can't say the same for some of the other PCO's. You would get ribbed mercilessly if it dropped on your watch. Also, if the seal fell off and you had to go out when the President was on stage. You would have to purchase a case of beer for the team. Of course, we never drank until the mission was over and the President left.

DAILY INTELLIGENCE SUMMARY

One of the most important things and scariest things I did was handled the daily National Intelligence Summary (InSum) report. I will not go in-depth on this topic because of its classification. But, the President would get a report every day that compiles intelligence information and other information from all the different governmental agencies, all in one report. My team made only two copies of this document every day, one for the President and one for the National Security Advisor. The only one that could see the full report was the PCO on duty, who had the clearance to see all this information in one place. Our job was to count the pages and make sure all the pages were in the report and that the report was consolidated into one documents before giving it to the President and the NSA representative. Sometimes a page would be smudged or was not clear and we would have to go back to the place were that page came from and get another copy. I never read the whole report cover to cover. I did not want to know the information that was in that document, but on occasion while reviewing it to make sure it was complete and readable you had no choice but to read somethings. I was amazed at the depth and width of items in this report.

We would number these reports #1 and #2 and would provide them to the appropriate person in the morning. Later in the afternoon we would try and retrieve both reports as to destroy them by the end of day. While on the road, off The White House grounds trying to find were the reports ended up could be very complicated. We never knew where the President or NSA rep would level the InSum report, in the Limo, or on AF1, or in event hold room location. It was the PCOs responsibility to find the InSum report before anyone else. Because of this very reason the Secret Service would not release a location from being secure, even after the President left a location until the PCO went in and searched that location for the InSum. The Secret Service would always want us to hurry up and release them and we would always say hold on we have to clear the space first.

I had found the InSum on a couch in a hotel room, on the Limo seat, in a Presidential hold room and many other places. You would think the President would take better care of this highly classified Intelligence Summary report and hand it back to the PCO when he was done with it. But, no that was not what happened, the PCO played hide and seek to find and destroy the InSum. It wasn't really the President fault, he was always being pulling from one thing to the next, his time was not his own. He was a busy man.

The PCO always found the InSum and destroyed in a timely fashion. The PCOs I worked with and trained with were the most professional, dedicated, patriotic people you ever met. This also goes for the surrounding military and Secret Service that supported the President. They all took every mission they were given very seriously.

TRAINING FOR AN EMERGENCY

The military and the Secret Service worked hand in hand when it came to the safety of the President and the continuity of Government that included the Executive Branch. We would all train repeatedly for that day we all hoped would never come, an emergency event involving the President.

We trained for all types of emergency scenarios and had a plan for almost everything. I love watching TV or movies that show The White House being attacked. I would just smile saying to myself that would never happen because we already worked through that scenario and would have done XYZ to stop that. There are contingency plans on top of contingency plans and we trained on these over and over again. In most cases, The White House staff and even the President did not know these plans. It was up to the Secret

Service to keep the President alive and safe and it was up to the Military to ensure that the continuity of the Executive Branch stayed in tacked.

EMERGENCY TRAINING AT THE WHITE HOUSE

All the emergency training we did in and around The White House was when the President was out of town. One weekend when I was working at The White House and the President was out of town, I was asked by the Secret Service to participate in an emergency exercise. I jumped at the chance and said, "Yes." The Secret Service agent briefed me on the exercise and handed me a sign that I put around my neck. The sign said, "President" and had a picture of President Clinton on it. I was instructed to go to the Oval office and have a seat. I sat down in the Oval office on the couch that faced the Rose Garden. I could not bring myself to sit behind the President's desk. It was a once in a life time opportunity, but I just couldn't. I was just sitting in the Oval Office looked out the window, waiting for the exercise to begin. How many people can say that sentence?

All of a sudden, an alarm went off and you could hear gun fire (blanks). It was a weekend with the President out of town, no staffers in the office, no press in the Press Pool area. We had The White House all to ourselves to play these exercise scenarios. After a minute or so, several Secret Service agents burst into the Oval Office and grabbed me. They physically moved me, almost picked me up off my feet, out to the South Lawn. By the time we made it to the South Lawn a helicopter was landing. Several other folks with signs around their necks were right there with me and we were all rushed onto the helicopter and it took off.

Wow, what a rush, to see the Secret Service, and the military support all react professionally and quickly to a threat. I will not go into more detail about the what's and how's of this exercise, but I was in awe of how quickly things happened.

I was thrown into the Presidents seat on the helicopter. Other roll players with name signs around their necks were trying to get on the helicopter at this time. Per the plan the Secret Service agents would not let them on. There are only so many seats on a helicopter. There is an order of precedence of who gets on and who gets left behind. It was surprising to realize that in an emergency some very important people are left behind. This was all part of the training for the Secret Service agents. They must only allow the right people on the helicopter and must be forceful to powerful people to keep them off. Only people with assigned seat get on.

As we flew off the South Lawn and I looked down, I could see the people we left behind. I just had to smile, knowing those individuals in real life would be getting a dose of reality. They would just be realizing that they really were not as important as they thought they were. We flew off the South Lawn faster than I had ever seen a helicopter take off before. We flew low and very fast to an undisclosed location. A plane was waiting for us at the end of a runway with it engines running and ready to go. We got off the helicopter and ran across the tarmac to the stairs of the plane. Before we could even sit down the plan was taking off. I will not go into the timing or the what's or how's but needless to say what a rush. It took no time at all and I was in the air and could be going anywhere in the world.

I saw first-hand how these professional Secret Service agents and military personnel are ready to do their job. These professionals knew what to do, how to do it and just did it. It was amazing that the as the President in this scenario, I did not have a say in what was going on. I was just a watchful participate to the saving of my own life and the continuity of the office.

TRAINING FOR ANOTHER DAY AT THE OFFICE

The Secret Service and military support personnel did a lot of trained off The White House grounds. We would train in all different types of scenarios like; motorcade emergencies, speaking event emergencies, and airport emergencies. Each one of these scenarios had different types of responses for different types of threats. We would train on them over and over again until we knew our duties inside and out for each threat.

In my very first training scenario, I was again asked to stand in for the President. This scenario was a standard airport arrival event. They always liked putting the new guy in as the President to observe the training, before you are incorporated into the training event. There I was standing at the top of a set of stairs next to an aircraft with a sign around my neck saying "President." I was waving at the crowd. We had people standing in as reporters and a rope line of spectators.

As I was at the top of the stairs waving, all of a sudden multiple stun grenades and other pyrotechnics went off.

This was to simulate the attack from a group of bad guys shooting at us with mortars from across the airfield. It was amazing, the Secret Service agents reacted to the very first sound of gunfire and ordinance. They figured out were the bad guys were and at the same time kept an eye out for all the people playing civilian. The Secret Service Counter Assault Team (CAT) in black fatigues came out of the woodwork and started returning fire (with blanks). They laid down such suppressive fire that even if the bad guys were wearing kevlar vest there would be no way to survive the counter fire coming from the Secret Service. You never see these CAT agents at a regular event but they are there out of site always watching.

I don't know where all the Secret Service agents came from but they were all over laying down suppressive fire. Other agents came from nowhere and grabbed me and threw me in the limo to speed away. This particular scenario did not stop at the airport attack, because as soon as we went down the road in the limo the motorcade got attacked.

At the end of the scenario we would have an after-action review to go over what went well what did not go well and how to improve. We were standing at the base of the plane running through the scenario as part of the after-action review. When I noted that there was no place to stand, without standing on bullet shell casings. There were thousands of casings on the ground. I don't ever remember the Secret Service agents reloading but I do remember there was never a lag in suppressive gunfire. These Secret Serve agents were good, they knew firing disciple, they worked in teams so there was always someone shooting lead downrange when the partner agent was reloading. They also had enough ammo left from the first attack at the plane, for the second attack on the limo. That is what training does for you, work at the problem, come up with solutions and then test your solution. This was great training, a full day of working different scenarios. I played different parts as spectators and role players. I also received training during the scenarios learning inside and

out what a Presidential Communications Officers does during an emergency event.

I was lucky enough never to have to use this training. But each PCO was always ready to support our nation if it came to that. I was so impressed with the outstanding professionals that I trained with and worked with on a daily basis. These professionals give of themselves every day, both training and executing the mission, to support your way of life, by supporting our government. These professionals are not the ones you hear about in the news. You don't see them up front in the cameras. No, they are the ones behind the scenes just doing their jobs in an outstanding manner.

CHAPTER 6
My Not So Normal
Work Day

Working day after day at The White House could really get to a person. The stress was un-describable. But there were times when working in the people's house was inspiring.

THE COMMUTE

My day started every morning around 5:00 A.M. when I would get up and get on the road to drive into the Washington, District of Columbia (D.C.). We lived in Lakeridge, Virginia, south of the metro D.C. down Interstate 95 (I-95). This was the best place for my family, good schools, and a lot to do for the family. But what was good for the family was not so good for my commute into the city. What a way to start the day, with the stress of driving with millions of other people into the city.

I would have to drive I-95 up to D.C. every morning. On the up side, I-95 had some High Occupancy Vehicle (HOV) lanes that had limited access on and off of them. The HOV lanes went one way into the city in the morning and reversed and came out of the city in the afternoon. These special HOV lanes were only for people that had three people in their car during the rush hour. But were open to anyone before 6:00 A.M. in the morning. I got up every morning to use the HOV lanes before 6:00 A.M. If I was late and didn't make it onto the lanes by 6:00 A.M. I would have to drive in the stop and go traffic on 1-95. A second option was to stop and pickup people waiting for a ride share. There were parking lots off of I-95 for people that didn't want to drive themselves to D.C. People would stop by these parking lots and pickup ride share strangers to get three people in your car so they could use the HOV lanes. When you got into town you would drop these folks off at several predesignated locations in the city. I did not like picking up ride share strangers but would do it if I wanted to get into town fast.

In the afternoon, the HOV lanes would open up to all traffic at 6:00 P.M. on the dot. Before 6:00 P.M. the police would pull you over if you didn't have three people in your car. But at 6:00 P.M. and after you could drive with just one person in your car and use these limited access HOV lanes. The skill here was to leave your office at just the right time to hit the HOV lane entrance just at 6:00 P.M. If you're early you would get a ticket, if you were over ten minutes late the HOV lanes would be just as crowded as the normal lanes.

Traffic in the whole metro area was a real mess and always crowded. If that was not bad enough, while I was driving these roads they started road construction on the I-95 and I-285 interchange and the Woodrow Wilson Bridge over the Potomac. Both of which I had to go through almost every day. All this construction made the traffic worse. After commuting in D.C. traffic for over four years, I never complained about commuting anywhere else.

THE OFFICES

I had several different offices that I worked out of depending on what I was doing that day. My primary office was at The White House Communications Agency

(WHCA) Headquarters building on the Naval Support Facility Anacostia (today it's called Joint Base Anacostia-Bolling). This was where I Commanded the Data Systems Unit from running all the Information Technology for The White House. I tried to get to this office every week day. I loved going to see the people that worked for me, that kept the Date Center going, that handled all the communications. This was also the location that my folks did most of their training and I enjoyed participating in that. My command support staff were based here and my boss (who also had several offices) tried to work out of the WHCA Headquarters as much as possible. But the Anacostia location was just one of my many offices.

I had another office on The White House grounds that I very rarely used. Space was very limited in this area, so I let whoever was my teams Shift Leader use that office. I only had a few of my personal and work items at that office. I tried very hard to make that office generic so anyone on my team could use it.

I also had a good number of my people working in the Situation Room under the West Wing. I did not have an office in the Situation Room but I did have a desk space with my name on it. Again, I would let the Shift Leader that worked for me use that space. It made no sense to have these work spaces kept empty in hopes I would come by to use them.

I had a good number of my people that worked twenty-four hours a day, 7 days a week, 365 days a year (24/7/365) in places in and around The White House grounds. I can't get into what all my military members did. But no matter what time of day or night I always had someone working for me on The White House grounds. I wanted them to know I was thinking of them, so I would surprise them by showing up at 4:00 or 5:00 A.M. in the morning with some donuts and coffee. I was an early morning person and loved to go in early to see the night shift. With so many folks that worked for me doing shift work, I never got a chance to have a military formation or group meeting with all my people it one place at one time. Someone was always working or traveling. I made it my mission to meet all my people, but to do that I had to make an effort to meet them in their work space when they were on duty.

My boss knew that out of all the leaders working for him, I had the most personnel in the most locations. But he was still amazed at how I got around so much between the 18 Acres and all my other locations. I was always on the move visiting my folks, asking them how they were and what I could do for them.

Another office I used a lot was The White House Communications Agency Operations office over in the Old Executive Office Building on The White House grounds. They always had an open desk for any WHCA officer on duty. Sometimes I would work out of The White House Military Office or the Military Aides office both in the East Wing.

I spent about half my time on the 18 Acres of The White House grounds and the other half of my time at Naval Support Facility Anacostia at the WHCA Headquarters office. Our Anacostia office was classified in the old days. Today I just looked on Google maps and the building that is The White House Communications Agency is shown. Boy times have changed.

PARKING

Parking in D.C. is an adventure. Parking around The White House is almost impossible. The Mall area has a lot of short term parking for tourists, but that doesn't work well if you are working at The White House. You would have to run out every two hours to feed the meters. There are some parking spaces for White House employees around the Presidents Park and the Ellipse Park just south of The White House South Lawn. These parking spaces are all by permit only. No permit and you get towed. The White House Commutations Agency only had one parking permit for Ellipse Park. This one parking permit was for the on duty Presidential Communications Officer (PCO). When you were coming on duty as the PCO and arrived at the parking space you would call the PCO coming off duty. They would have someone else come out to the space and move their car so you could park. They would hand you the permit tag that you would put on your rearview mirror. Then you would run into the office and do your shift hand off, as the friend would stay with the other car so it didn't get towed. We had to do this dance every day. It wasn't to bad since we changed shift early in the morning before most of the civilians were coming into work. There were usually a few open spots to pull into and wait until we would get all the cars moved around.

The best way for the military personnel to get to work at The White House was to take the metro/subway. We also had a White House Communications Agency shuttle that would take you back and forth between The White House and the WHCA Headquarters in Anacostia. This way if you had equipment to carry you would just drive to Anacostia and park in the secure lot at WHCA. The shuttle driver would come over to your car and you could load whatever you needed. Then get driven right through the gate onto the 18 Acres. With my job and having so many folks all over the place using the shuttle was great, I could go back and forth from The White House and WHCA Headquarters all day long depending on what was going on and where I needed to be. The down side was parking at Anacostia added more time to my commute and made for some long days in traffic trying to get home.

ALMOST RUNNING OVER HILLARY

Parking is an issue in downtown D.C. especially around the 18 Acres. Even more of an issue is parking within the 18 Acres grounds itself. There are a limited number of parking spaces inside The White House grounds. All these parking spaces are designated for specific purposes, for specific vehicles. As the Presidential Communications Officer we had a specific purposed vehicle that we kept on The White House grounds. We always wanted to make sure the batteries and the engine were in tip top conditions, so we swapped out this vehicle once a week or so for a maintenance check.

It was my turn to swap out the PCO vehicle and drive it onto The White House grounds. I made it through the Secret Service vehicle security gate after showing my identifications and have the vehicle checked. I was driving between The White House on the east and the Old Executive Office Building on my west, inside The White House compound. One of the rules when you are moving a vehicle inside The White House compound is to move it to where it needs to go and park as quickly as possible. The

Secret Service don't like moving vehicles so closely to the West Wing.

My parking space was up a vehicle ramp to my left and into the center court yard of the Old Executive Office Building. Everyone knows that you are suppose to get out of the way of a vehicle so it can park right away. But when I turned to go up the ramp there was a crowd of people all in a big circle not paying attention to me and my car. I kept edging forward and some of the people on the outside of the circle started moving to the side to let me pass. I continue to move forward slowly. I got to the point where there was this one lady with her back to me just not moving at all. My bumper was all the way up to her legs, so I finally honked the horn, with a little beep.

Well you can guess who the person was that was just ignoring me? It was the First Lady, Hillary Clinton. After I honked my horn, she turned around and looked at me. I thought she was going to yell at me, just like she was yelling at everyone else in the group. But, instead she just glared at me and moved to the side to let me pass. When I drove passed by, I heard her yelling to the group about something or another. I went by and the group reformed around the first lady to continue to get scolded by her.

From then on, every time we had an issue with the First Lady. My team would remind me, all that I had to do was hit the gas when she was in front of me. Then all the crap we had to deal with from the First Lady would have been over. Hillary provided me and my team a lot of stress over the years. It was very hard to be a service provider to the First Family, they treated me and my team like servants. Always demanding, never thanking and it wasn't just my team they treated like this, it was everyone.

STRESS and REDUCING STRESS

Writing this book has reminded me of how much stress I was under when at The White House. As a PCO being responsible for the last link of communications between the President of the United States and the National Military Command Authority was stressful enough. Add to that, my full-time job as the Commander of the Data Systems Unit had a no-fault tolerance for Information Technology. Most IT jobs in the civilian sector look to have a five 9's uptime, that means being up and operating 99.999% of the time. But being the Chief Information Officer at The White House required a seven 9's up time (99.99999%). What that means is that the IT system could never be down. Never have an outage. Never cut over to a new system and have a hick up. It didn't matter if it was the middle of the night or the weekend. My team had to be perfect in their Information Technology support mission. We all knew how important our jobs where and how important our mission was. We lived this mission everyday working our no-fault tolerance jobs. One mistake and you would be fired and your military career would be over.

The job I was hired into was a two-year long joint military tour. They did not expect military officers to take on this kind of stress and pressure for more than that. I happened to stay for four and a half years. I was asked to stay after my first two-year tour and then again after the end of second two-year tour. I finally raised my hand and said it was time for me to go at the four-and-a-half-year time frame.

When I arrived at The White House, I had a nice short blonde hair cut. When I left The White House four and a half years later all my hair had turned gray from the stress. The same can be said for every President, they come into the job with a full head of colored hair and they all leave with gray hair. The stress of The White House will turn anyone's hair gray.

One thing I did for me to try and reduce my stress level was to run. I worked so much that I ended up only being able to run every other or every third day. But I would get out and run as much as I could. I would both run while I was in D.C. and if I could on the days we traveled.

I got with a few other co-workers and we would all try to go running at lunch time if you could get away. Exercising like this in the middle of the day gave you a lot more energy in the afternoon and help you get through the day. It got to the point that we were all getting in really good running shape. A group of us decided to start training for the Marine Corps Marathon, that they held right there in D.C. every year.

When we ran at lunch time, we would be running from The White House up the mall to the Capital, around the Capital, down the Mall and across the bridge to the Pentagon, around the Pentagon and then back to The White House. Our runs got longer and longer every week. At one point we needed to run longer routes. So, then we would start from the WHCA Headquarters building on the Anacostia Navy grounds and run up across the Anacostia river bridge to the Mall area and then all the way to the Pentagon and then to Arlington Cemetery and back past The White House and the Capital and back to Anacostia.

Our one-hour lunches started turning into two-hour lunches then two and half hour lunches. The closer we got to the

Marine Corps Marathon date the longer our runs would take. I loved running in downtown D.C. there was so much to see, so many national monuments, the people, the tourist, running up and down the Mall, running up the steps of the Capital on one end and running up the steps of the Lincoln Memorial on the other end.

With all this running, I felt in the best shape of my life, even though I was in this incredibly stressful job. With all that running and training, my friends and I ran the Marine Corps Marathon with no problem. I had one of my best finishes ever for a marathon. I had done several other marathons earlier in my life but now I was over 40 and I felt like I was in better shape than when I was in my 20's. We decided to keep training and running and do the marathon again the following year.

My boss found out that several of us were doing all this running at lunch time and that we ran the Marine Corps Marathon one year. He also found out that we were going to do it again the following year and try to get even better times. Well that went out the window, not the running, but the getting better times. Vice President, Al Gore, decided he was going to run the Marine Corps Marathon the following year. My buddies and I were detailed to the USSS to help with security for VP during the run. We had to run at VP Gores pace, which was considerably slower than our own pace. We ran in a group providing mobile security for the VP during the race.

We did all this running and getting ready for the Marine Corp Marathon each year. Out of the four years in D.C. I was actually only able to run the Marathon twice once on my own and once with the VP the other two years I was traveling with The White House and missed the race.

However, we did do four Army 10 Miler races in. The Army 10 Miler was also run in D.C.

I always thought the exercising I did while at The White House was a major reason for my ability to deal with the stress of the job, for over four years. Another way I was able to deal with the stress was the outstanding people that I had working for me. I had the best military people in the world working for me and they knew there jobs very well. This was a major stress reducer to, because I knew I didn't have to micro-manage them, they could do their job, with or without me.

HMX1 AND THE SOUTH LAWN

One of the neat things I got to do was to work with the HMX-1 Marine helicopter squadron. You see when you want to land a helicopter on the South Lawn of The White House you can't just come in and land. That is not a safe way to do business. A helicopter pilot cannot see under or behind his helicopter. You need a pair of eyes on the ground looking under and behind for you. My team and I were the ones that provided that on the ground support for landing and taking off of the Marine helicopter on the South Lawn.

We had equipment that provided us control like a miniature control tower. We would keep this equipment storage in an area off the Diplomatic Reception Rooms, on the lower level of The White House. This was a lecture size piece of equipment on rollers, that we could just be rolled out to a location where you had full view of the South Lawn. This equipment had a weather station giving us all the pertinent weather data that we could relay to the helicopter. We also had noise canceling headphones and microphone so we could talk to the helicopter, air traffic control, and the Secret Service. We provided ground safety/security for the landing and provided weather/wind information also.

Helicopter landing under the control of my team

When we knew a helicopter was coming in for a landing we would roll out our equipment and stand by. We would also notify The White House grounds personnel. They would roll out three very large round plywood disks onto the green grass and set them down on the ground for the Helicopters wheels to land on. The lawn had three coffee lids nailed down in the specific location for the helicopter wheels to land on. The large round plywood disks would be rolled out and put right on top of the nailed down coffee lids. This helped with the grass not getting all messed up with the weight of the helicopter, especially when the grass was wet.

The helicopter pilots could see the large round plywood circles on the grass. These plywood circles were painted red with a very big white X in the middle. The pilots could see them from the sky and vector to land right on top of them. The press and any other people watching from the South Lawn entrance could not see these plywood circles because of the angle of the yard and where they were standing.

Getting ready Presidential departure, me talking with the press to test sound quality

MEETING NEAT PEOPLE

One of the benefits working at The White House was you get to meet some special people. I am not talking celebrates, sure they are around the President and The White House all the time. During the 1996 Presidential Campaign, you saw tons of celebrates at fundraisers and other events.

One of the special people I had the honor to meet and talk to were a couple of Tuskegee Airmen. They had come to The White House for a ceremony and I was there escort. I meet them at the guard gate and gave them a VIP tour of The White House grounds. I had the honor of talking to these great men, showing them around, and listing to their stories of WWII.

I was so impressed with the Tuskegee Airmen that I went to my boss and asked him if I could put together a Professional Development program for our whole unit and have the Tuskegee Airmen come back and talk to our troops (Soldiers, Airmen, Sailors, Marines, and Coast Guard). I wanted our young men and women to know what it really meant to give it your all, to go against all odds and not only surviving but to thrive.

I was able to get six Tuskegee Airmen to come back and talk to several hundred of our young troops. They talked about discrimination, segregation, World War II, and not only surviving but being one of the best units. This was done through leadership, through unity and through keeping up their moral as a unit. All these important lessons are still needed in today's military. These men were humble, in recounting the history they lived. These men were also old and would not be with us for much longer. I am so happy that they were able to pass on their history and their knowledge to our younger generation of military members.

I had a chance to meet a lot of other humble, smart, and special people at The White House, this is only one example of many.

MY NIGHTS AT THE WHITE HOUSE

As a Presidential Communications Officer (PCO) I had to be in very close proximity of the President while I was on duty. That meant when the President was in The White House, I was in The White House. If the President slept the night at The White House when I was on duty I had to sleep at The White House that night too. I spent a lot of time at The White House, being ready for that emergency that I hoped would never come.

As I mentioned in the previous chapter about the "Four Horsemen," there were four of us that had to stay with the President all the time, to include during the nights. Each of the Four Horsemen would spent our time differently. I like going around and talking with my people that were working shift on The White House grounds. I also like walking around The White House at night. It would be 10:00 P.M. or 11:00 P.M. and all of the day time workers would have gone home. The only people around would be the Secret Service agents and some of the twenty-four-hour operations type folks. Most of which worked for me in IT and Communications areas.

I walked the dark quite hallways of The White House at night all alone. I would look all the items on display throughout The White House. I would go to the Red Room, or the Diplomatic Reception Room, or the Library. It was really nice at that time of night when it was quiet, with all that history there to read and soak up. I enjoyed talking to the Secret Service agents on duty and get to know them. I would read all the signs on all the historical items and help teach myself more and more about The

White House. I learned so much about the history and items within The White House that I was often asked to give VIP tours (see Chapter 11).

I loved to walk out to the Jacqueline Kennedy Garden between The White House and the East Wing and sit on a bench and eat my dinner. Or maybe go over to the Rose Garden between The White House and the West Wing and sit there just looking out at the lite up Washington Monument. I would just think of all the history around me. It was awe-inspiring to think about the others that had sat in that same place before me.

The Secret Service agents that guarded this section of The White House got to know me very well. I would always take my meals outside to one of the gardens and sit there and feeling in the history while I was eating. On the weekends, I loved eating my lunch outside during the day and watch all the people on the other side of the fence looking in at The White House. I just knew I was having an experience that most Americas would never have and I wanted to try and soak it all in.

Not only did I walk The White House at night, listen for the old ghost of the past. But I also had to actually sleep the night at The White House. Everyone asks me if I stayed in the Lincoln Bedroom, no I did not. I never went up to the residence floor of The White House, where the First Family slept. I stayed down on the working levels of The White House and I slept down in the bunker. The bunker under The White House had several rooms in for sleeping. The Military Aide and I were usually the only two of the Four Horseman that actually spent the night in the bunker. The Doc had a nice office in the ground floor of The White House and would usually stay there. The SAC would usually be up all-night handling security issues and would switch off with another SAC in the morning. The bunker room I stayed in was the size of a prison cell maybe six feet by six feet with a single bed and a very small table with my communications gear on it. This was no Lincoln Bedroom and there was no valet service. It was military living in an austere environment. But I am not complaining how many other people can say that they slept at The White House? Not many.

OTHER THINGS THAT HAPPEN AT NIGHT

One night, when I was the PCO and was down in my bunker room getting ready to go to sleep. All of a sudden, I heard the internal Secret Service alarm system go off and I heard over the radio the Secret Service jumping in to action. They had caught an intruder that had climbed over the fence onto the South Lawn. I wanted to see what was going on, so I went up and got the full story from the Secret Service agent in charge and was just amazed at what I found out. The Uniformed Secret Service Agents had caught a young, very drunk, Marine in civilian clothes on the South Lawn zig-zagging around trying to find his way around. They had also caught two more young, very drunk, Marines in civilian clothes on the outside of the South Lawn fence and now all three of these Marines were in handcuffs waiting for their Commander to come get them.

It seemed that all three Marines were out on the town drinking and were all smashed. The two older (not by much) Marines thought it would be great to play a trick on their younger buddy. They told their buddy that The White House fence was the Marine barracks fence. That they were returning late and if they go through the gate they would get in trouble for being so drunk and late. The fence around The White House is exactly the same type of fence that is around the Marine Barracks area on "8th" & "I" streets, across the mall and down some from where The White House is. One guy jumped the fence and was wondering around the South Lawn looking for his Barracks building. The poor guy was tackled by the Secret Service before he could get to far.

The guys outside the fence were laughing so hard when their buddy got tackled that the Secret Service outside the fence just walked up to them. Asked them what they were doing and they explained the joke to the Secret Service agents not understanding that they would get in trouble too. This is only one story of many that happen at night around the 18 Acres.

SOCKS & BUDDY – THE PETS

Sometimes at night I would run into the Clinton's pet cat, Socks. This cat had the run of The White House and the grounds. Most of the time he was kept up in the residence, but every now and then he would get out and roam the property. Anyone that saw Socks would pick him up and take him to their office for a while until Socks wanted to go somewhere else. It was like everyone that worked at The White House had adopted Socks. Socks was a male domestic short-haired cat that was a stray that jumped into Chelsea's arms back in Little Rock. He ended up getting adopted by the Clintons and came to The White House with them.

One night at 1:00 A.M. when I was pulling PCO duty and sleeping in the bunker, Socks jumped up on my bed and on to my face. I could not imagen how that cat got into a highly secure area with all its doors and security features. I got up, picked up Socks, and went over to where my team worked. Went I walked into my teams work space I found them having a birthday party, for one of the guys on shift that night. Socks had followed one of the guys carrying the birthday cake. I am sure Socks was hoping he would drop some food. Socks had been invited into the bunker to come to the party. That darn cat got into everywhere.

I found out that my people brought the cat over to my area. They had put Socks in my room as a prank and to get me up for the party. I just had to smile, these small pranks were part of what the night shift did all the time. Small harmless pranks helped you release stress. I didn't mind, it was all in good fun. It did put a smile on my face and cake in my stomach. We took Socks out of the secure area later that evening so he could continue its nights prowl.

Me with Socks

I did run into Socks one other time of note, this was in the secretary's office outside the Oval Office. We were getting ready to set up the Oval Office for a televised speech by the President. We had all our equipment in the outer office waiting for the President to finish whatever he was doing at the time. I had about 50 lbs. of equipment that I was holding and I was getting tired so, I sat down on one of the chairs in the corner of the office. I sat down hard, I was tired and the equipment I was holding was heavy.

As soon as I hit the seat I knew I sat on something. I immediately got back up and noticed I had sat down right on top of Socks the cat. He blended right into the color of the seat and I just didn't see him sitting there. I looked at the cat and it was not moving at all. The first thing that got in my head was "Oh My God I sat on Socks and killed it." What was I going to say to the President when he opens the door in a minute? I poked at the cat and it didn't move, I felt for the lungs to move up and down and I could not feel anything. I lifted up the cat's head and looked right into its face and the eyes were shut and it didn't move. I thought I had killed the First Family's pet. I knew that I was a goner now!

But right then right when, I was going to say something to get help, that fat, old cat, just got up stretched, jumped down from the chair, curled up underneath it and went back to sleep. I guess that cat was roaming the grounds all night and had just started his night of sleep. Well at least I didn't kill it. I was safe with my job for a little while longer.

The Clinton's never took care of Socks. Every one else ended up taking care of Socks. Socks mostly hung out in the secretary's offices. Then finally in 1997 when Buddy the dog came on the scene Betty Currie the Presidents

Secretary ended up adopting the cat. Socks and Buddy did not get along at all.

Buddy was a male Labrador Retriever that the Clinton's adopted in December 1997 as a holiday gift for the family. He was only three months old when he came to The White House. This presented a problem for the Secret Service and the household staff. As the Clinton's didn't have time to potty train Buddy and to take him for walks. This was left to the household staff and or the Secret Service. This was always a bone of contention for the Secret Service that a well-trained security professional, became a dog walker.

MANIPULATING THE PRESS

I learned a tremendous amount about politics and the press while I was at The White House. I was in a very non-political position, providing Information Technology and Communications. I provided a service to The White House and its staff. They needed that service even during some of their very political discussions. I was not a threat, because I was a military officer doing my duty to support the Commander-in-Chief. I did not have any party affiliation. Since I was not a threat, I was often in the proximity of many conversations that were very private between the President and his staff.

What amazed me the most was during both the Travelgate investigation (1995-98) and the Monica Lewinsky (1997-98) investigation, the way The White House and the President manipulated the press. It seemed to be very easy to do. The White House knew the press wanted a story, they also knew how to give the press the story that they wanted to tell. The White House knew if they leaked a piece of information one way, through a senator, that senator usually used ABC reported in XYZ media and that editor usually slants the story this way or that. They also knew that if they leaked something through a different congressman, then that congressman usually used ABC reporter in XYZ media and that editor usually slanted the story in a specific way.

With this type of knowledge, The White House could manipulate the press and have the story slanted in the best light for The White House as possible. They could control the message, they could control what was on the 5:00 P.M. or 6:00 P.M. or 11:00 P.M. news. These news reporters all thought they were the ones getting the scoop that they would win a Pulitzer for their investigating reporting, but that was just Bull Shit. The White House was the puppet master letting the information out the best way they could to get the story they wanted.

The press at times did find something out that was not in the original White House message, but The White House would just change the message once that piece of information was known.

There is no more "Free" press, every press organization out there wants the most sensational news they can get. It's all about ratings. The more viewers the higher the ratings and the more that station can charge for their commercials. The news media uses teasers before each commercial to make you come back, to watch their station. It's all about the news cycles today, what new news do you have to save for the next news cycle, what can separate your news organization from all the others. They are all fighting for the same scrapes of information that are being fed to them by the politicians, who know how to manipulate the message.

I know I now have a very cynical view point about the press and about politicians. But I have seen and experienced all this first hand. I got so good at understanding what was going on at The White House, that I would come home and tell my wife "Watch NBC tonight at 7:00 P.M." or "Read the Washington Post Evening addition – first page." I was almost always right at what station would have that new piece of information before the other stations.

This is not a Republic thing or a Democratic thing. Both sides do this every day, all the time. It was amazing to me that the politicians and the news reporters were all out for themselves. There was no one out for the truth. The truth was not sensational enough and didn't get the ratings they wanted. It was all about the five to ten second sound bites and who got to that sound bite first and then move on to the next sensation sound bite. When is the last time you heard a news, broadcast start the broadcast with an apology for something they said that was wrong? I think the answer is never. Apologizing for ruining someone's life is not important and sensational enough to start off the news with. An apology will be hidden at the end somewhere.

By the way the American people are really at fault for this type of media reporting. The American people want sensationalism. They want immediate news, right now. They want short sound bites. They want to watch FOX and CNN and the other news media outlets. They want to take everything they hear for the truth, without doing any research on their own, without questing what they are hearing.

Be an informed consumer, question what you hear, question why, look for the rest of the story. There are always two sides to every story, is the news media you are listing to giving you both sides?

HILLARY AND THE LAPTOP

This book is not about politics, this book is not about democrats or republicans. But how can I tell a story about The White House without talking about the Clintons? My opinion of the First Lady was formed early on during my time at The White House. Then this opinion was revalidated over and over again during my many years working in close proximity of the Clintons.

I will put it right up-front the First Lady and I did not get along. It is my opinion no one really got along with Hillary Clinton. I found her to be rude, she treated me and my team as menial servants, was two faced, lied, and all in all not a nice person.

One of my first interaction with Hilary was when I was on duty at The White House during the day about a month or so into my job there. I was in charge of all the Information Technology (IT) used by The White House, that included the laptops used by the Presidential family. This included Chelsey's laptop that she used for school.

One day Chelsey came home from school and told the Secret Service agent she was having a problem with her laptop and needed some IT support to fix the issue. She had a report that needed to be completed that evening and needed her laptop. The Secret Service agent on duty called the IT helpdesk. The IT helpdesk, called me since they knew I was on the 18 Acres and asked me what I wanted to do.

146

Chelsey had gone up to the residence on the upper floors of The White House. It was very rare for anyone on the support staff to be able to go up to the residence. I looked at who was on duty on my IT team at the 18 Acres and found a senior IT enlisted person that had been working at The White House for over twelve years. I called this person and told him to go up to the residence and help Chelsey with her laptop issue. This was a big deal since the IT and communications team that I ran almost never got called to go up to the residence. My IT guy ran across the 18 Acres and told the Secret Service agent he was there to help with the laptop. Then he took the elevator up to the resident floor to help Chelsey.

It only took him about fifteen minutes to fix the issue and was walking down the back staircase from the residence to the working floors of The White House. Who does he run into coming up the stairs but the First Lady. Hillary just started yelling at my technician. She didn't give him a chance to say anything, to explain, to answer any questions, no she just laid into him. Who are you? What are you doing here? You know no one is allowed up in the Residence? Just yelling at him and then said "Get out of my site." My technician made it down to the bottom of the stairs and asked the Secret Service agent to use the phone and tried to call me. He couldn't get me right away, it took him a minute or two to track me down and get me to a phone where we could talk (remember these were the days before everyone having a cellphone).

My technician started to giving me a briefing on what had happened with the First Lady. He also told me What he had to do to fix Chelsey's laptop. Before I got off the phone with my technician, The White House operator cut in and told me that the Commander of The White House Military Office wanted to see me in his office right now. I double timed it over to the East Wing where the WHMO is and reported to the Commander. He told me that Hillary wanted the IT technician that was up in the residence fired right there on the spot and removed from The White House.

I knew the First Lady was just in The White House Usher Office (The Ushers Office – handles all the personal needs of the First Family and the residential floor along with running The White House Staff), asking questions about something or other. We did not inform the Ushers Office that my technician went up to the residence since the First Lady was in with him and they were busy. Since we didn't inform the usher he did not know to inform the First Lady. But, my technician was going to pay the price for not following the process of informing the Usher Office before going up to the residence.

The technician that I had selected was going to retire in six months with over twenty years of distinguished military service, having spent twelve years at The White House. I was not going to let Hillary ruin his outstanding military career for just doing his job. I told the Commander of the White House Military Office that this was not fair. It wasn't fair that Hillary would not listen to anyone about this issue and would not give us any ability to explain what happened. She just wanted this technician gone and gone today. I told the Commander that if it was anyone's fault it was mine and if anyone would be let go it should be me. I offered up my resignation then and there, but my Commander would not accept it.

We worked together to come up with an idea of what to do to help this soldier. After all he was only doing his job, the job we asked him to do. I called the soldier and told him to go home for the day and to stay home for the next couple of days. We decided that we would have the soldier go on the road when Hillary was in The White House. Then come home and work on the 18 Acres when Hillary was traveling. This outstanding soldier did exactly what we asked of him for the next six months and retired without a blemish on his record.

The First Lady was like this a lot she would just go off the handle all the time at the littlest thing. It really got worse during the Monica scandal. The First Lady knew how to turn on and off her personality, to show people what they wanted to see. She would have made a good actress, because that is all she ever showed the public, an act! The public never really got to see the real Hillary, only those that worked the inner circle got to see the real her.

Ok, Hillary Clinton had a few good traits and skills. But I knew the real Hillary Clinton and, in my opinion, she was not a nice person. Again, in my opinion, from what I saw, she was, manipulative, condescending, arrogant, and was most of the time a real b____ (you fill in the word)!

CHAPTER 7
PCO Travel and Support

When the President was traveling outside The White House grounds he depended on the same outstanding military support he had on The White House grounds. This meant my team and I traveled with the President everywhere. During these trips I had a lot more interaction with the President and his staff. With all that interaction came a lot of interesting stories that you will read through this book.

THE TACKLE

At all the events the President goes to there are a lot of tasks that need to be accomplished to support that event. I was participating in my very first in town event and was learning these tasks of what my team did. As I mentioned in a previous chapter the new Presidential Communications Officer (PCO) is always given the easy jobs to learn first. This allows him/her to get over the butterflies and nervousness. It was my turn to be the new PCO. I was given an easy assignment, to call over the radio the Presidents had arrived at the event location. I would stand in the loading dock area and wait for the limo to pull in. The loading dock doors would close and then I would call arrival over the radio. I would say something like, "Eagle Arrived Washington Hotel." This way everyone in the motorcade or at the event site could hear over the radio that the President was in the building. Calling arrival was an easy task to do and that is why as the new PCO I was given this task.

Well, at this particular event I was told that we were shorthanded and I would have to do multiple tasks. I was asked to also hang the Presidential Seal on the podium indicating that the President was in the building. This is another easy task for a new PCO to do. I was happy to do both it would give me more experience. Then I asked the question if I am at the loading dock and the podium was on the other side of the building how would I be able to do both tasks at the same time?

The person that was training me said that would be no problem. The President was going to a holding room to meet some people first. I had plenty of time to run from the loading dock to the other end of the building to hang the seal. I could run through the back hallways and get to the stage. No one would be in my way because the back hallways were clear of people. The Secret Service kept the hallways clear for security reasons.

It was at my first in town event, I had tasks to accomplish, I had things to learn, I was becoming part of the team. I was pumped (maybe pumped a little too much as you will see). This would be the first time I would meet the President up close since starting at The White House. I was ready to go and knew I could do these easy tasks with no sweat. After all, look at me I was one of the best, I was hired to work at The White House, I was someone important or so I was beginning to think.

The President arrived at the loading dock, the limo pulled in, the Secret Service closed the loading dock door. There I was just feet away from the limo and the President. I did my job, I used my radio and called "Eagle arrived Washington Hotel." This let everyone know that the President was in the hotel. Right after I called arrival, as the President was getting out of the limo the PCO training me pulled me aside and started to quiz me on my tasks. Did I call arrival correctly and what I was supposed to do next? I was so nervous at the questioning, I thought I had messed up, but I hadn't. I answered all his questions correctly and was beginning to think, this stuff is easy what is the big deal? Then my trainer reminded me I had to go hang the seal on the podium and that I better get going. I had to get to the other end of the building as quickly as possible. I started to jog down the back hallway to get to the other end of the hotel, to the stage area. We had an offstage area where the seal was.

It was the Secret Services job to keep the emergency exits routes clear of people, this included the back hallway. But here I was coming up to a gaggle of people in the hallway blocking my way. I was so focused about my task, that I just pushed my way through these people. Pushing them to one side or the other. I ran into a tall guy in the middle of the group and knocked him down. I had a mission to do and these folks were in my way. I told myself, I would talk to the Secret Service later and chastise them for not keeping the emergency exit clear of people.

I arrived at the back of the stage in what I thought was plenty of time. The people from the motorcade and the President where not there yet. I grabbed the seal from the offstage area, calmly walked out on stage and hung the seal on the podium. The sounds and tone of the people in the ballroom instantly changed, seeing the seal on the podium, knowing now that the President was in the hotel and would soon be on stage. I went back to the offstage announce area. This is where me or one of my team would make the offstage announcement of the President and his guest onto the stage. I was standing at the offstage announce area, looking at the announcement cards to make sure there were no last-minute changes.

Right then a tall man put his hand on my shoulder and said "You looked to be in an awful rush – did you get done what you needed to do?" I turned around to meet the President, face to face, for the first time! I looked at this person in front of me and realized exactly who I had knocked down in the hallway just a couple of minutes ago. I had not realized that the President was a big tall guy until right then. I thought to myself, Oh My God, I had knocked the President of the United States on his butt. I was going to get fired, I just knew it! I responded to the President "Yes sir," letting him know I had completed my task.

I looked over the Presidents shoulder to the Secret Service agent in charge and the PCO that was supposed to be training me. They were both laughing their heads off. As a side note, you never see a Secret Service agent laugh on duty, especially when the President is around. But here these two were covering their mouths and laughing hard. I don't think the President knew anything about the trick that the team played on me, the rookie PCO.

The President was in a very good mood this particular day and just looked at me and said "Let's go, do the announce." They had set me up, played a trick on the new guy. They had taken me down a couple of notches. Made sure my head wouldn't swell up to big in this new role at The White House. At the same time, they taught me some great lessons. Be ready for anything, because anything can and will happen, you need to plan for that. You not only need to learn your job, but you need to learn all the jobs of all the people around you. It is a team effort to provide security and support to the President. Everyone needs to be a part of that team, not an individual.

I didn't get fired and I never knocked the President down again. I did accumulate many other funny stories' like this one, that are in this book.

RUNNING WITH THE FOOTBALL

As mentioned in Chapter 5 there are always four people "The Four Horsemen" with the President at all times. I was one of the Four Horsemen and the Military Aide was another one. Since we worked so much together I got to really know the Military Aides. We were both in the military, we had a lot of similar interests and experiences to talk about. We were together all the time when traveling with the President. We covered for each other all the time too, that helped both of us get the mission done.

I remember one event very well, when I helped cover for the Military Aide. We were doing an intown event where the President was going to speak at a hotel about three blocks from The White House. Even though this event was just three blocks from The White House, the President couldn't just walk down the street to get there. There where to many security concerns for that. So, a motorcade was used to travel the three blocks to the hotel. This event was nothing special, a standard thirty minute or so speech for the President.

This was a small old hotel, with not a lot of room for all The White House support staff. The Military Aide and I just stayed in the loading dock area and hung out by the limo. It was a nice sunny hot mid-summer day in D.C. The Military Aide and I had gone for a very long run earlier in the day. We had both been drinking a lot to try and re-hydrating our fluids all morning.

We were standing around waiting for the President to finish his speech and for our return to The White House. When the Military Aide told me, he had to go to the bathroom bad. He couldn't wait until we got back to The White House. He said it would only take him a minute and that he would be right back. No problem the President was suppose to be on stage for a little longer and then he usually stayed around shaking hands and talking to people. We were all use to what we called "Clinton Time." He was never on schedule, always late, always did whatever he wanted to do no matter what the schedule said. We were all use to this and just lived with it.

The Military Aide said, "I am going to the bathroom, call me on the radio if the Presidents status changes." I said, "Ok, I will call if anything comes up." As I mentioned before the Military Aide always cares the Presidential satchel, or as it is better known "The Nuclear Football" with him. So, off the Military Aide went to find a bathroom carrying the "Football." No big deal we had time and then you add on that "Clinton Time," we would be there for a while.

Well it wasn't five minutes later that I heard over the radio that the President was moving to the limo to leave. The President for some reason was hot to get back to The White House. He went from leaving the stage straight to the limo and said, "Let's go." The Secret Service said that everyone was not back in the motorcade. That the staff and The White House Press Pool were not loaded back up yet. The President didn't care we were only a few blocks from The

White House and he wanted to go. He told the Secret Service lets go, they can follow later or walk.

I tried to call the Military Aide on the radio but he wasn't answering. This was an old building built with solid thick walls. I found out later that the bathroom the Military Aide went to was in the basement of the building. I continued to call the Military Aide on the radio over and over again. I started by using proper radio procedures "We have an imminent departure by Eagle." I did not hear anything from the Military Aide on the radio, but I did hear everyone else calling on the radio to scramble to get to the motorcade. All the staff and press ran out of the building to the motorcade and jumped in the cars. The President was getting upset and told the Secret Service, "Let's go now!"

The motorcade took off to go back to The White House with no Military Aide and no Nuclear Football. I kept trying to call the Military Aide on the radio and finally I just threw out proper radio procedures and called the Military Aide on the non-secure channel by name. The non-secure channel has more power and greater range then the normal encrypted channels. All of a sudden, I heard the Military Aide on the radio responding. I told him the motorcade had already left the hotel and left him behind. I heard a couple of four letter words come over the radio.

The motorcade had left the hotel with me in the last vehicle of the motorcade. The front of the motorcade had already made it the three blocks to The White House gate and were entering the South Lawn drive, when I got a hold of the Military Aide. When the last vehicle, the one I was in, of the motorcade came to The White House gate, I jumped out and stopped to talk to the Uniformed Secret Service agent at the gate. I asked him to keep the gate open for a second or two. He asked me why? I pointed down the street towards the hotel that we just left. All of a sudden you saw a man in full military uniform come out of the hotel running like a mad man. He was wearing his military jacket with all his ribbons and badges on it. In his hands were his military hat and a large briefcase. He was moving fast holding up that large briefcase with both hands across his chest. He looked like a quarterback running with a (very large) football down a football field. But instead of a football field he was running down the middle of Pennsylvania Avenue. The street was still closed off by the police because of the Presidential motorcade. The Uniformed Secret Service agent at the gate and I were laughing out loud at the Military Aide trying to catch up to the motorcade. Trying to get back to where he was supposed to be, next to the President. It was one of the funniest things I ever saw. Seeing the Military Aide, in full uniform, running down the middle of Pennsylvania Avenue, with the Capital in the background, and all these cops that had the road closed looking at him with the "Nuclear Football" in his arms.

The Military Aide made it to the gate after a couple of minutes of running down the road. After thanking the Secret Service agent for holding the gate, we both turned and walked up the South Lawn drive to the motorcade. The Press and Staff where in the process of unloaded from the motorcade. For some reason the President had not gotten out of the limo yet. He must have been on a phone call in the limo. The Military Aide and I walked up past the limo right when the President was getting out. He took one look at the Military Aide and asked him what was the matter? The Military Aide was sweating profusely, all out of breath, and his face was flush. Both the Military Aide and I said, "No problem Mr. President" and just went on our way.

But, we both knew for a couple of minutes that the "Nuclear Football" and the President were separated. The United States was a risk for those brief minutes. The Football was always supposed to be next to the President twenty-four hours a day, seven days a week, 365 days a year. Even though it was very funny watching the Military Aide running down the middle of Pennsylvania Avenue in full uniform with the "Nuclear Football." We both knew that this was a big incident that just happened. But we both decided not to report this event. You are hearing about it right now for the first time.

OUT OF TOWN TRAVEL

Going out of town presented a large logistical challenge in supporting The White House. But the military was up for this challenge. After all this is what the military does deploy military members all over the world, setting up bases in distant lands. However, traveling with The White House had a lot of perks that we didn't have when we were deploying to the field while in the service.

Most of the out of town travel was accomplished by flying on military cargo aircraft, both my people and our equipment to include our mobile communications platform called the "Road Runner." The Air Force supported The White House with aircraft so much that they had special designations for the air support missions. The Air Force called any Special Air Missions (SAMs) in support of the President, "Phoenix Banner" missions. They called the Vice President SAM missions "Phoenix Silver" missions. The Airforce kept both aircraft and aircrews on standby to support short notice Phoenix Banner and Phoenix Silver missions. These SAM missions in support of the President were some of the highest priority missions for the Air Force and received a lot of special attention.

When we traveled out of town we would start by loading our equipment out of our warehouse in our Headquarters building at the Anacostia Navy Yard. We would load our equipment onto trucks and drive our equipment out to Andrews Airforce Base. There we would off load the equipment out of the trucks and onto military aircraft pallets. The onloading and offloading was all done by hand. Everyone pitched in no matter what their rank was. Handling our equipment this way was manpower intensive but it was all part of the job. We would offload at the other end in much the same way, using manpower to move our equipment around and into rental trucks.

We had to bring all our own equipment when traveling to support the President. We had specialized radio, communications, and information technology equipment that was secure and classified. On a typical in country short trip we would take a small cargo aircraft, like a C-130. We would only have two or three pallets of equipment and our Road Runner vehicle. On an overseas trip we would fill up a large cargo aircraft, like a C-5. We would have around twenty pallets of equipment, several vehicles, and a large generator, depending on where we were going.

We always tried to send an advance team ahead of us, that would fly commercial and meet us at the airport. This advance team would get the rental vehicles (trucks/vans/cars) and have them waiting for us at the airport. The advance team took care of a lot of the logistics on the ground so that when the plane landed with all our equipment we just went to work for the upcoming Presidential visit.

After the trip was over, we would recover all our equipment, box it back up, and leave for the airport. At the airport an Air Force cargo plane would be waiting for us to load our equipment onto. We would leave the rental cars/vans/trucks at the airport on the ramp for someone else to pick up and we would head home.

AIRPORT OPERATIONS

With the President's use of Air Force One as his primary means of mobility, we did a lot of airport operations. When we flew into a city to set up that location for a Presidential visit we would often landed and unloaded our equipment at the same airport that the President and Air Force One would use.

We did a lot of coordination with several different groups on the airport grounds to make a Presidential trip happen. One of the groups we coordinated with was the Airport Fire Department. We would ask the Fire Department to park their fire department trucks outside on the fire department ramp. So, the Secret Service could store the Presidential Limo in the enclosed bays. We would some time store some of our equipment and our Road Runner vehicle at the Fire Department too. This gave us an automatic secure facility with bathrooms and sleeping quarters at each airport. My team would put a secure White House phone in the Fire Department. That way the Secret Service could guard the equipment and vehicles until they were gone, with secure communications.

One of the other things we would do is to go up to the tower and put a secure White House phone there. This tower line was for the Secret Service to use during the Presidents arrival and departure. My White House badge could get me access to almost any area of the airport and that included the FAA control tower.

Another thing we would do at the airport was to get the telephone company to provide us with several telephone lines at the closes building to were Air Force One would park. The Air Force advance person would complete an airport site survey to locate the spot were Air Force One would park. He would mark the parking spot on the tarmac. After the Air Force One person would mark the parking spot, I would make sure that I had a telephone cable long enough to reach that spot from the closest building. We would preposition a several hundred-foot roll of telephone cable from the building and run that cable across the tarmac to the noise wheel of Air Force One.

When Air Force One landed, there would be two people standing out on the tarmac. The Air Force One advance person to vector Air Force One onto the parking spot. Then there was me right next to him with the telephone cable. When Air Force One stopped, I would walk up to the front nose wheel. On the nose wheel of Air Force One was a telephone box that I would open and plug in the telephone cable into. This provided a secure landline phone capability for the time the aircraft was on the ground. When Air Force One was ready to leave I would unplug this cable and close the phone box on the noise wheel. Then I would have to quickly reel up the phone cable across the tarmac before Air Force One would start moving. The airport position is one of the first positions you learn as a Presidential Communications Officer, because it is the easiest position to learn. While it was the easiest position to learn there was still a lot of pressure to make sure you got it right.

One of the things about the airport position that made it very hard was the unwritten rule about being in press photos. While working as a military member in support of the President there was an unwritten rule not to get your face in any press pictures. We were supposed to be in the background, be support personnel, and not be seen. If you got your picture in the newspaper or on TV you would have to buy a case of beer for the team after the mission was over. This unwritten rule made the airport position the hardest duty to have, because the press was always at the airport to film the arrival of the President. When the portable stairs were pushed up to the front nose of Air Force One, the front wheel with the telephone box on it was right in the press shot. You had to be very careful where you stood and moved under Air Force One behind the stairs to stay out of the pictures.

Out of all the times I was the airport PCO and plugged in Air Force One, I was only caught on camera once during the Presidential campaign in 1996. But on those back to back campaign stops several other of the PCO's got caught on camera too. At the end of the campaign we had a big party and we all split the cost. I had a great time thanking our team members who all had worked so hard during the 1996 re-election campaign. It was a great party.

EMERGENCY PREPARATIONS

Being ready for any emergency situation is one of the primary missions of the Military that support The White

House. My team would not just set up one way to communicate, but we would provide multiple ways. A primary, a backup and another backup at every location the President went to. It was a lot of work to set all this communications at every stop, every location, every event, but that was our mission.

The team would setup multiple communications not only at event sites but along the whole motorcade route. We would work with the Secret Service to make sure we knew both the primary and backup motorcade routes. We would take our communications equipment to buildings along the motorcade routes and we would use our White House badges to get us to the top of those building. We would use the utility or maintenance rooms on the top of these buildings and put our equipment in these rooms. We would put tamper proof seals on the equipment boxes and chain the equipment in place. We would setup our equipment all over the city to support a Presidential trip.

We would also work with the Secret Service for the emergency medical facilities that would be used. We would put in a secure White House phone in the emergency rooms of all the medical facilities that may be needed. A Secret Service officer would man these phones during the visit.

We would work with the HMX1 helicopter team to cover the normal landing zones and the backup landing zones with communications just like the motorcade routes and the event locations.

We would always be ready with a primary plan, and a back up plan on how to communicate securely anywhere the

President may possibly go in the host city. It was a lot of work every time the President traveled but that was our job.

HOTEL SETUP

When traveling in support of the President, whether it was in the United States or overseas we needed to setup some support offices for The White House Staff, the Secret Service and the Communications team. It was very common for us to use hotels with meeting rooms or a ballroom as our bases of operations. We could sleep, eat, and work in the same location with minimal travel. It was easier to keep one location secure for both sleeping and working. We would try and taking over the whole hotel if we could. But some hotels were just to big so we would just take over a couple of floors. Our offices would be in the ballrooms or meeting rooms. If the hotel layout for its meeting rooms was not secure enough we would use connecting bedrooms. We would have the beds moved out and tables and chairs moved in. If we used bedrooms for offices we would have our sleeping rooms both above and below the offices. Security was a big deal when we were on the road.

We did this everywhere we went, we had to have base of operations to work out of during a Presidential visit. We needed a place to meet, to do secure communications, and a place to rest that was safe and secure. Using Hotels like this was actually a great way to have everything in one place. But to get the space we needed in hotels you had to plan ahead to get hotels with the space and requirements we needed. At The White House there was a travel office that was responsible for planning for hotels and for long-range travel plans. The President's schedule normally was planned weeks in advance. During the Campaign the scheduled changed a lot almost daily, but the base of operations or hotels had to stay the same as much as possible even if the Presidents scheduled changed.

My team would setup and tear down equipment for every trip and every location. There was a lot of manual labor each time we moved. But that was the way we had to do business. We would carry microwave dishes up to the roof of hotels with no elevators. We would carry telephone switches with us. Set them up in the hotel and hook them up to landlines that we ordered. We would set up a fully functional White House switch board room. Along with rooms for the Secret Service operations center and a set of White House staff offices.

My team was great, no one complained and everyone pitched in no matter your rank or your duty position. Everyone helped unload, setup, at the end tear down and pack up. Some time it would take us weeks to setup and test all our equipment. But when we tore down in would only take hours. I ruined many suits pants at the end of an event because I pitched in to help pack up everything right after an event. I learned to bring a change of clothes with me, but a lot of times I didn't take time to change. After an event we all wanted to just get out of there as fast as we could. I would always take off my jacket and set it aside. But I would ruin the pants helping pack up. I finally learned to purchase two or three pair of pants for each suit jacket I got.

THE IMPOSSIBLE IS POSSIBLE WITH A BLACK CARD

Every now and then the President put a last-minute pop-up trip on the calendar. This usually happens when there is a natural disaster like a hurricane or flood. These last-minute trips usually happen a day or two after the disaster. There is little to no lead time to do all the things we normally do around communications, security, and planning. All our normal planning and lead time goes out the window. But nothing changes from a support and security requirement. We still have to make the trip happen, just faster with less planning.

The way this type of pop-up trip would happen was The White House Staff or the President would give the Secret Service and us a twenty-four-hour notice that he wanted to go somewhere. We always had a small team on standby, for various reason and this was one of those reasons. That team would be given notice and be in the air usually within two hours, with an already pre-packed set of equipment. While the team was in the air in route to the disaster site the operational team in D.C. would start coordinating with FEMA and the local Federal and State folks on the ground. It is a big deal to take the President into a disaster area, the support structure and security structure have already been devastated by the disaster. You don't want to pull away needed resources doing search and recovery operations just for a Presidential visit.

One time I was on the standby team, when a hurricane hit hard with a lot of flooding. The President decided to go show his face in the disaster area. We got the call and were told to be wheels up in two hours. We landed at a small airport about thirty miles outside of the disaster area. The airport and the area around we were at had power, and water and was mostly undamaged. I got on the phone and called back to White House operations. They told me that they contacted a nearby hotel that we would use as our base of operations hotel. Because of the need for quick set up and security they had coordinated us to take over the hotel for a couple of days. The hotel was full with displaced individuals from the disaster, but The White House had coordinated to move everyone out of the hotel. These people could move back in after we left which was usually just a day or two.

I showed up at the hotel front lobby to meet with the manager and the Secret Service agent in charge. We told him that we would be taking over the hotel and answered all his questions and got to work. The Secret Service would sweep the hotel and then put up a secure perimeter. My team would take over the meeting room areas and the ball room. We started setting up offices for The White House staff, the Secret Service and my own team needs. We kept the fact that we were with the President and The White House as close hold as possible. It was good operational security not to tell anyone who we were. All people knew was we were with government. It was vital for security that we didn't let anyone have any planning time if they wanted to do something against the President.

While we were unpacking and setting up work spaces at the hotel. The operations team back in D.C. would contact the federal representative of the local telephone company. They would coordinate to have the local field supervisor meet me at the hotel. This was always the fun part for me, and it also showed the weight and power of the federal government. The local field supervisor would come and meet me. He would always say there is a disaster in his area and all his teams are working the disaster. He would say that since we already had phones in the hotel there was no need for his teams to come and provide more lines at the time of this disaster. Because of operational security I could not tell him we were with The White House and we needed these phone lines for the President.

It was always the same story from the local telephone representatives, they were in charge of their area and no one would tell them how to do their job. That is until I said "Call this number." I would provide a number provided to me by D.C. Operations. The local representative would call the number and a very high-ranking person from their own company, like the President of the company, would answer the call. They would call the local representative by name and say do whatever Agent Gelhardt tells you to do and to make it happen fast. They were always surprised by how high up this went and that we knew all about him, his name, his job, his boss, etc. The long arm of the federal government in full swing.

I would tell him I needed a 200-pair trunk line run to the hotel ballroom and that I needed all the lines active in twelve hours. They would say that is impossible he didn't have the crews left on his team to do this work, with the disaster going on. All his crews where already out. I would ask, "What do you need?' He would say something like, "I need five trucks and fifteen technicians that would have to work straight through a twelve-hour shift." I would say, "Ok let's get it done." He would ask how are we going to get this done and who is going to pay for this?

I would take out a black American Express card and tell him that this card would cover all the cost.

When I joined The White House, I was handed a black American Express card. I had never seen one of these cards before. I asked what the black card was for? I was told it was for anything that I needed to meet the mission, from equipment, resources, food, etc. It was my responsibility to use the card correctly and I had to sign a couple of pieces of paper with the guidelines for the card. There were all types of government guidelines that I had to follow. I asked what was the limit on the card and I was told it did not have a limit. I asked what was the level of oversight for the card? When and how would I be questions about it use. I was told unless I charged over a million on the card no one would really question my use of the card. I didn't understand at the time I received the card, but as you can see from this story, it was a well needed tool for the mission.

I told the telephone representative that this card would cover all expenses and all he had to do is provide an itemizing bill. He was impressed and ask who I was and what agency I was with, but I couldn't tell him. What I could do is give him another phone number for the federal representative for AT&T. They talked about the local needs for people and equipment. Within an hour or so the people and equipment showed up.

There are emergency stocks piles all over the United States for many of the infrastructure areas like power and phone. You just have to know who has them and where they are. My operations guys in D.C. knew all the right people to call to get things done.

The telephone technicians worked through the night running the lines to where we needed them. We would attach the lines to our own traveling White House switch with our own encryptions and classified capabilities. We would have a mobile White House in a day and meet the mission for the President.

At the end of this event, the phone representative handed me an itemized bill for a lot and I just handed him my black card. With the weight of the government and a black card, we met mission! We provided support for the President when he came to the disaster location and the public got to see their President supporting the country.

HILLARY'S REACTION TO THE MONICA SCANDAL

I do not want to besmirch Ms. Monica Lewinsky and that is not what this story is about. Ms. Lewinsky was young and impressionable person working at The White House. The President was memorizing, very personable, and after all he was the President. The scandal that came out of their sexual relationship affected more than just the Clinton Family. The scandal affected the whole White House and the support needed to the First Family. The increase in support to the Clintons costed the taxpayers additional money that most people are not aware of. Also, what the public saw had no place in the reality of what was going on behind closed doors. Let me give you just one example of many:

The President and the First Lady stopped at Elmendorf Air Force Base, Anchorage, Alaska, in November of 1996, on their way back from the APEC Summit in Asia. This was supposed to be a refueling stop and during the refueling the President was going to talk to a hanger full of military members and their families. I was part of the advance team setup for the event. My team and I worked with The White House Staff all the time at all types of event, but this event was different.

The Monica story was not yet in full swing at this time, but we all knew something very big was up. The First Lady – Hillary was not happy at all and was barley talking to her husband (President Clinton). She had sent her own First Lady advance person for the stop in Alaska. So, we had two different White House staff people we had to make happy, the Presidents and the First Ladies. I didn't mind this, we work with difficult people all the time, but I was amazed at some of the ridiculous demands from the First Lady's team.

The first one was that the First Lady would not ride in the same limo with the President. We tried to explain that since this was an event on a military base and that the president was only traveling half a mile from the terminal to a hanger just down the tarmac that we had only brought one limo instead of the normal two (primary and a backup). The First Lady's team didn't want to hear this and told us to get a second limo. We had to fly in a second limo just for the First Lady.

We were planning on using the largest hanger on the Airbase for the President's speech to the troops and families, that way we could get more people into the event. When we did the site visit and looked over the hanger there was only one office available in the hanger. We would often use office space for the President as a hold area. This gives him a space with a secure phone, go to the bathroom, talk to his staff, and for security to have a spot that the Secret Service can secure. Well with the largest hanger, only having one really good office space, the First Lady's team dis-approved of this location. We had to find a hanger that had two connected office spaces so the First Lady could have her own office location to be in. We were told that she would not share any space with her husband. We had to move the event over a couple hangers and the base commander had to clean out a second hanger and area for the event. The base commander asked us why we would not be using the larger hanger so more of his troops could attend. I didn't have a good answer for him, I just said that was what The White House wanted.

We were ready for the event, Air Force One landed and the motorcade with two limo's in it made it the half mile or so the hanger. The President came in and went to his hold location, the office we had setup for him. The First Lady came in after the President and went to her hold location, the office we had setup for her. They did not talk, they did not look at each other. It was so bad that the staff of the two teams didn't even talk to each other. My team and I ended up being in the middle of everything.

When it was time to go out on stage for the speech to the troops, we had to go to one staff and tell them it was time, then we had to go to the other staff and tell them it was time. The two of them, Bill and Hillary came out to the center section between the two offices and didn't look at each other or talk to each other. They were both talking to their staff people and ignoring the other. We pushed the two staffs, the President, and First Lady to right behind the curtain on the side of the stage.

It was amazing, right before they could be seen by anyone on stage or the audience, they turned grabbed each other's hands started smiling and stepped out from behind the curtain. They both started waving to the crowd on the floor and to the military on the stage like they were a happily married couple. The President gave his speech with Hillary right by his side the whole time. It was a relatively short speech for the President and then they both shook the hands of the military members on the stage. Then they grabbed each other's hands and smiled and waved to the audience and walked off stage.

It didn't take more than a couple of steps behind the curtain before Hillary let go of Bill's hand and went off to her own hold office space with a scowl on her face. The President went off on his own hold office space not looking to happy either. These two were great actors, no one in that audience could have noticed that this was a family greatly divided. All they saw is what the Clinton's wanted them to see a smiling waving President and First Lady. Again, what actors. Back to Air Force One in the two separate limos.

AIR FORCE ONE - A NEAR DISASTER

When Air Force One landed in Elmendorf Air Force Base, Anchorage, Alaska, in November of 1996, and a second plane (The White House Press Plane) landed there also. Both planes were on their way back from the APEC Summit in Asia. This was a refueling stop for both planes while the President did a speech to the military on the base.

As a side note every time Air Force One goes overseas there usually is a second plane for the large group of press covering the Presidents overseas trip. The Press Plane usually takes off after Air Force One, taking pictures of Air Force One departure. Then flies past Air Force One in the air and lands at the next location before it, so the press can get off the plane and be ready to take pictures of Air Force Ones arrival.

In Elmendorf the Press Plane landed first, the press got off and were ready for Air Force One's arrival. Air Force One and the Press Plane landed late in the day when the sun was still up. The planes landed right before a large snow storm rolled in. After all, it was November in Alaska and the weather can turn bad really quickly. When the planes landed, the tarmac was clean and dry and there were no issues at all with taxing to their parking spots.

The President, his staff and the press (in the second plane) all got off the aircrafts and went to a very large hanger down the flight line. The President was giving a speech to a hanger full of military and family members there at the base. After the speech, everyone went back to Air Force One and the Press Plane to get ready to take off.

By the time we had gotten back to the planes, a ton of snow had fallen. They had brought out the snow plows and the plan de-icing equipment. They were plowing the taxi way and runway as fast as they could. The sun had gone down and it was getting colder fast. The weather front that came in must have been a cold front that came through brining the snow in so fast. The snow on the ground that wasn't plowed off the tarmac had started to melt because of the tarmac was still warm from the sunny day. But, just as the snow melted the cold wind from the front would come by and freeze it to ice.

The whole tarmac was nothing but a big sheet of ice now. Walking from the motorcade to the airplanes, felt like you were out on an ice skating rink. The planes were ready they had been de-iced, fueled, and everyone was loaded up. I was on the ground watching as Air Force One started powering up its engines and started to move. Because of the snow on all the taxi ways Air Force One had to turn around and go to the one open taxi way they had plowed.

As a rule, when Air Force One was moving on an airfield no other planes moved. This is called a ground stop for the airfield. This happens at every airport that Air Force One comes to whether it be a commercial or military airport. Just imagine what happens when Air Force One lands at an airport like Atlanta's, Hartfield-Jackson International airport, the busiest airport in the world. Every single plane on the ground has to stop in place and not move for the full time Air Force One is on its inbound leg to the airport and while it is taxing to its final spot. This causes havoc to the schedule at any airport Air Force One goes to.

The same ground stop was in affect at Elmendorf Air Force Base. The press plane could not move until Air Force One was off the ground. Air Force One was turning around using its engines to push itself around in the space on the tarmac that was plowed clean. But by now that same place which was just plowed clean now had a sheet of ice all over it. It took some power for Air Force One to get moving and to turn in the space it had. As big and heavy as Air Force One is, it started to slide on the ice on the tarmac. It slid past the initial turn that was needed and kept sliding towards the Press Plane on the ramp. The Press Plane had not started its engines yet, it could not do anything even if it wanted to. You could hear the engines of Air Force One straining to reverse engines and try to stop the skid. But Air Force One keep moving towards the Press Plane sliding across the tarmac.

All of the people watching this from the ground knew the two planes were going to hit. The wing tips were only a few feet away from each other, full with fuel. This was a disaster of huge proportions just about to happen right in front of our eyes and there was nothing any of us could do! But as luck would have it that day, Air Force One just slide by the Press Plane with just a couple of inches between the wing tips. Air Force One just kept going, taxied and took off. I wonder if the Air Force One pilot even knew how close the two planes had gotten?

MARTHA'S VINYARD -
THE SCANDAL CONTINUES

Most of the time when we traveled with The White House, it was for short-term events or speeches. When we did those events, we were always working, every day from the day we got on the ground to the day we left. We would be setting things up, working the events, and then taking things down. The only exception to this rule was when the President and First Family went on vacation to specific locations where we kept things set up.

I was selected to be the Presidential Communications Officer for the Clinton's trip to Martha's Vineyard in August of 1998. I felt so lucky, this was the first vacation trip I had ever been picked to work. When we went to specific vacation spot all the pre-work was already done, all the surveys and locations for our equipment, etc. All we had to do is turn everything back on and put in the updated encryption software into our communications equipment that was already on the island. I was so looking forward to the planned several days of just relaxing. This was supposed to be the easiest thing we did, support a vacation. I was looking forward to the low stress of vacation support. But that was not to be on this trip to Martha's Vineyard.

The President had just admitted, on 17 August 1998, about his inappropriate relationship with Ms. Monica Lewinsky. This trip was to be a "Healing the hurt" vacation within his family. But the First Lady was mad as hell the whole trip. Every time I was around all I heard was Hillary yelling at Bill and at times throwing things at him. It was like being around a fighting cat and dog going at it over and over again for twelve straight days. There was no vacation time on this trip. You never knew if something you said or did would sent Hillary off. We were all walking around on egg shells every time you had to be around the First Family.

So, what was supposed to be an easy trip for me ended up being one of the most stressful trips I had ever been on. I could not wait to go back to the normal stress and grind of working an eighteen-hour day at The White House.

CHAPTER 8
On the Campaign Trail

I joined The White House at the end of 1995 and there was an election year right around the corner in 1996. One of the most difficult time working at The White House was during the Presidential campaign because of the operational tempo, with an unbelievable amount of travel and campaign stops too numerous to count. But, we supported the President, not as a candidate, but as the leader of the Executive branch of the United States, that still needed to run the country even during the campaign season.

DEALING WITH SEPARATION OF DUTIES

During a campaign there are a lot of volunteers and political party personnel that are trying to get things done quickly, with changes happening every day during the campaign cycle. Part of what the Presidential Communications Officer had to do is to educate all these non-White House personnel on what the White House Communications Agency could do and what was outside of our responsibilities. This could be very confusing to the campaign personnel that didn't deal with The White House all the time. All the different Presidential support teams on the road had the same issue of educating the campaign personnel that we did. The support for the President was as "The President" not as a candidate running for an office. We were not supposed to be taking sides, to help one political party over the other, that was not our job. Our job was only to support the current President to do his White House duties not his campaigning.

An example of this is, the White House Communications Agency (WHCA) put out hard line telephones at different locations for the use of The White House Staff and the President – not for the use of the Democratic campaign personnel. We would have signs next to each phone saying, "This Telephone is For OFFICIAL White House USE ONLY."

Sign we put next to each phone

As part of our White House communications duties we would install phone lines at every event site. The campaign personnel would ask if we could help them out with the campaign phones, with the phone technicians to put in the phones and then troubleshoot them when they were not working. Of course, we would have to say, "No, we can't help, we are only authorized to work White House issues." This was an ongoing battle throughout the whole campaign.

Another example would be the motorcades, there was a standard package of vehicles in a Presidential motorcade and the White House Communications Agency provided radio communications. During the campaign there would be additional vehicles for campaign personnel to get from point A to point B. But my team was not responsible to provide radios or any communications for campaign vehicles. We would get yelled at all the time by the campaign people for not providing communications for them.

This went on the whole campaign with new campaign volunteers at each site and reeducating these people over and over again. The White House staff that traveled with us knew the rules but they too would ask us to bend/stretch the rules over and over again. They would go to the individual WHCA technician on the ground just doing his job and ask for a favor. This would get out of hand and things would always get elevated to me as the Presidential Communications Office in charge. I would end up having to play politics and be nice and find a compromise to not piss off The White House full time staff but still stay within our legal boundaries of support. The last thing The White House would want, was to have a reporter see something shady going on and report it in the news the next day. The White House knew that and even though they would push for support most of the time they were reasonable enough to take "No we can't do that" for an answer.

PRESIDENT'S CAMPAIGN BUS AND TRAIN

One of the most unique things I worked on was how the White House Communications Agency would set up the Clinton campaign train and bus with mobile communications equipment. We set up two buses and two train cars with communications equipment, a primary and a backup bus and train. We set up self-tracking, self-leveling satellite communications that would be under a bubble on the top of the train or bus. We had to cut into the roof of the vehicles to make this happen. We ended up using a quarter of the back of the bus for our classified communications equipment, with a little door between our area and the rest of the bus where all the campaign people would be with the President.

The Presidential Train at a campaign stops that I worked

We also set up the bus with its own generator and the ability when we stopped to plug in landlines phone lines and landlines power. This gave us an ability to support mobile and when stopped it gave us primary and backup power and communications.

FUNDRAISING - MARTHA STEWART

As I mentioned the operational tempo of the campaign trail was unbelievable. We had two to four stops almost every day when the President was traveling. That was a lot of communication equipment and people to move around, covering every site that the President was campaigning at.

As an example of what we had to go through I will mention one event site that I was the Presidential Communications Officer in charge of. It was a fundraiser event at Martha Stewarts house/studio complex. At every Presidential event site, the Secret Service and the communication teams need space to meet our missions. This can cause a lot of disruption to an event host and the event itself.

Martha Stewarts house was a mansion with a good size film studio behind it and a very large yard. The White House support staff and others came in and started asking for changes from what was already planned by Ms. Stewarts. All the folks on Martha Stewart staff were telling us no, Ms. Stewart would not let us do this or that. It is my opinion that they were all scared of her, it seemed that she was a very demanding boss and no one questioned her way of doing things.

Well not me, I was not scared, I went right up to Ms. Stewart and starting telling her that we would have to change things for security and communications needs. She did not want to listen to me and told me, "That things would stay the way they were." I told her, "No they would not, if you wanted to have the President come to your house things would have to change." She was livid at me, asked me, "Who I thought I was," and that she would just call someone at The White House and get me removed from the site. I called The White House right in front of Ms. Stewart and handed her my cellphone and told her who was on the line. She started right in and told The White House she just couldn't work with me.

Can you guess what The White House said? Well they said, "Either comply with the site lead or the President would not be coming to this event." Martha was less then pleased. She would have to move her outside tent so the helicopters could land, she would have to change the schedule of events and the locations of the events to meet the security needs of the Secret Service.

HMX1 landing at Martha Stewarts lawn

I thought her house and studio were amazing but dealing with Ms. Stewart was less then pleasant. I was glad when that event was over with and we could leave.

We handled a lot of campaign events throughout the year. I was able to meet a lot of famous people some were nice, some were like Martha, all full of themselves. But I did learn a lot and see a lot during the campaign period. I learned a lot about the President skills during these events.

THE PRESIDENT'S MAD SKILL

During the campaign, I really saw President Clinton's outstanding skill sets. You don't get to be President of the United States without some skills and President Clinton had skills. You may have an opinion of his policies, you may like them or dislike them, but I would tell you unequivocally that he had some outstanding skills that were far above the average person. When it came to remembering things, being personable, and multi-tasking President Clinton was way above the average person. I witnessed firsthand on multiple occasions how President Clinton could remember things, multitask, and work people with a friendly smile and a handshake that made you feel like you were the only one in the room. There is no politics in what I am talking about here, just firsthand facts about President Clintons abilities that I saw with my own two eyes.

Let me give you two example of President Clintons memory abilities while on the campaign trail. During the campaign season which is almost a full year of campaigning starting in the beginning of 1996 and going all the way to the election day in November 1996 President Clinton was campaigning to get re-elected. We started the year in 1996 with a lot of fundraising events. It felt like we were doing something for the campaign every day or at least every other day. Some of these events were in town but many of them were out of town events.

One event that I witnessed firsthand was a photo opportunity in Boston with the President. People would pay money (something like $10,000) for a minute or two with the President to shake his hand and take a picture with the President. Most of these people brought their family and did group pictures with the President and their families. The campaign staff would setup all these photo opportunities with these high roller/rich donners. The staff would line everything up and the President would come into the city for one reason or another and would set aside an hour or so to do these photos.

The President would show up and go into the room that they were going to use for the photos. The photographer would be all setup with lighting and be ready to go. The President would walk into the room and almost immediately the staffer who organized the event would have a little biography card of the family and would talk to the President. These biography cards would have the names of the family the fathers first and last name the wife's first and last names, and the kid's names and ages and then something about the family that was a little personal piece of information. An example would be "Mr. President first you will be meeting with Mr. Jake Smith, President of XYZ company, in Boston and Mrs. Jacky Smith a house wife, they have two kids, Lily ten and Billy thirteen, Billy plays soccer and just made the game winning goal in last week's soccer game."

The family would then be escorted into the room the President would walk right up to them and get in their personal space and smile and shake hands and call them by their first name and congratulate the kids on whatever the personal piece of information was. He would do this so easily and no matter how rushed the President was on his schedule. He had the able to just make you feel like you were the most important person in the room, and that you and the President were old friends like he came over to your house all the time and knew everything about your family. He put the kids and the family at ease and then everyone turned to the camera and the photographer would take a picture or two and then the family would get ushered out. You would think that the president spent fifteen to twenty minutes with each family the way it went, but in reality, it was more like three to four minutes a family. They did this as an assembly line to make money for the campaign. The staffer would be in the Presidents ear as one family left the photoshoot telling the President about the next family.

I never saw the President make a mistake with someone's name, the kids names, or the special event. He did this, family after family for an hour going through 40 or 50 groups of people. It was simply amazing how he could make these very nervous family members be at ease, as if they were meeting their neighbor. This was a real skill to get personal with people and put them at ease. In about an hour of time the campaign could make half a million dollars just by doing these photo opportunities. The campaign did these photo sessions in almost every city we went to. What a way to make money.

It was amazing to see the President work the room and the people, but that is only half of this story. The rest of the story was when we went to another fundraiser about a month or so later. This was a $100,000 a plate dinner with the President. This was held at a wealthy donor's private home and there were four tables and the President would sit at each table for about a half hour. The eight people at the table would get the Presidents attention for that half hour while he was sitting at their table. This was high stacks politics, all business men in charge of big business.

One of the people there was there was the same Mr. Jake Smith that the President took a family picture with a month or so before. I was personally in the room when the President first met Mr. Smith a month ago, for some reason I also remembered this person. But the President remembered Mr. Smith from the photo opportunity in Boston, and this personal dinner was out west in California. The President remembered Mr. Smith's wife's name, the kids name and what the special event they talked about was. He asked Mr. Smith how his son was doing with his soccer and remembered every detail about their conversation a month earlier. How the President was able to do that after meeting so many people every day and shaking hands and taking pictures with all those high rollers. How did he remember this one person out of all the people he met?

Sure, you could say for some reason he knew this person or there was a connection with this one person. But, I personally saw the president do this over and over again, when he met people for a second or third time. He had the ability to remember everything about their last encounter. President Clinton had skills, mad memory skills.

Let me give you another example of President Clinton's multitasking and memory abilities. We were at a campaign stop in North Carolina. There were a couple of different events that the President was going to do at this stop. A photo opportunity, a speech on an outdoor stage, and another event I don't remember. This was going to be a quick in and out with Air Force One landing at the airport, a motorcade to the events and then back to Air Force One to fly back to D.C. The President was arriving from another city and he was behind schedule already on this day. Also, at this time, there was an international event going on that The White House was dealing with. This event caused the President to be behind schedule which was no surprise. As I mentioned before we were all use to "Clinton Time." The President did whatever he wanted, took whatever time he wanted, and it would always screw up the schedule. This impacted everything, like the closing of highways waiting for the motorcade and we would be fifteen or even thirty minutes late. The highway or interstate would be closed for thirty minutes for no reason other than the President was late. All of the Presidents travels were timed to the minute on what things would be done when. Like closing highways.

Here we were landing late and we were behind schedule, at the same time there was a world issue The White House was addressing. There was the President getting off Air Force One with a White House staffer in one ear telling him about the hot world issue that The White House was dealing with and asking how the President how he wanted to respond. In his other ear a local campaign staffer was telling the President about the schedule of events at this stop, who he was going to meet and what he was going to do. At the same time, the speech writer, who travels on Air

Force One, handed the President and updated speech for this event site, with the most up to date local information and incorporating comments about the current world issue that was going on.

Here is the President with a person in each ear and a brand-new speech he was just handed and he had to multitask all these things. He did all this without missing a beat. While we were in route to the first event, the President decided to cancel that event, and go straight to the outdoor speech event, to save time and to get the schedule back on track. We had to change the motorcade route on the fly and we showed up at the outdoor speech event more or less on time. The President was hustled up to the stage and was introduced almost right away. The thing of it is that the President was hustled to the stage so fast that the new speech that he was handed never made it from the limo to the stage in time. The military-aide and I had the speech in our hands standing offstage. We talked about walking onstage and putting the speech in front of the President. But as we were trying to make this decision, we were listing to what the President was saying and we were following along with the speech in our hand. You know what, the President gave that new speech he was just handed stepping off Air Force One, a couple of minutes ago almost word for word without the speech in front of him.

The man had people talking in both his ears on different topics as he was reading a new speech and just minute later he gave that speech almost word for word – that is mad skill sets of multi-tasking and remembering. You don't have to like the President, his policies or his party to still have a great reverence for the skills that got him into The White House.

THE FLAG CAPPER

Where I was very surprised to learn of the Presidents skills on the campaign trail. I was also amazed at all the folks around him during the campaign. There where tons of volunteers that wanted their ten seconds of fame with the President. I don't know how some of these folks ever passed the Secret Services background checks. It was amazing how many volunteers it took to run a campaign and handle all the events we were doing. Some of these folks thought they were very big in the campaign and came up with all sorts of ideas that The White House staff or military support personnel would have to shoot down.

Everyone always wanted some reminder of their part in the campaign. Whether that was a picture with the President or a poster used during the campaign or a Presidential napkin. People just wanted anything they could get their hands on and they took it. As I have mentioned before my team sets up equipment before an event and then takes it down after an event. This includes the Presidential Seal on the podium and the U.S. and Presidential Flag's used on stage, and many other things.

When my team was on the campaign trail with the President we were spread thin and didn't always have all the support and personnel we would normally have, but would still have to do all the same duties. At one event my guy that was in charge of the stage was also in charge of the audio video setup too. At the end of the event, after the President left and the crowd started clearing out, we started to pick up our equipment. Since my guy was up in the booth with the audio video team for this event, he started at that location picking up The White House equipment. It took him about thirty minutes to get down to the stage to start tearing that equipment down. When he got to the stage the Presidential Seal on the podium and the Presidential Flag was gone.

Me next to the Presidents and US Flags we traveled with

The Presidential Flags are handmade using real gold thread and are worth several thousand dollars apiece. The White House Communications Agency is responsible for the accountability of these flags while on the road away from The White House. As a side note the U.S. Flags and stands are a matching set to the Presidential Flag and stand, same size, shape, color, with the appropriate statues of an eagle on top of the pole. We travel with these matching sets so when the President gives a speech somewhere there are always matching flags behind him. We put these out because many event coordinators do not know the right way to show the American Flag, so we ensure that if the President is there the flags are done right.

My guy told the Secret Service right away that the flag and seal were missing. That started an immediate search of the area, of people still in the area and questioning of folks that may have seen who took the flag and seal. After about an hour we were able to figure out who took the items and the Secret Service told the local police to retrieve the missing Presidential equipment. The message that made it all the way down to the policeman on the end of this mission was very distorted. They were told that a person did something and had Presidential material. This became a very big deal for the locals. A police S.W.A.T. team hit the house of the person that took the flag and the seal. They broke in the door and swarmed the house and arrested everyone in the house.

Yes, the Presidential Flag was right there in the living room along with Presidential Seal on the mantelpiece over the fireplace. It was a volunteer campaign staff person that was helping with the event and thought it would make a good souvenir, he didn't ask anyone he just took the items. Now he had a federal warrant out after him for grand theft, he had a broken door and a lot of questions to answer. At the end of it all, the charges were dropped but this individual was banded from any Presidential events for life, by the Secret Service and he never again would get this close to the President and his stuff.

CHAPTER 9

Overseas Travel (Supporting the President)

Traveling overseas for The White House was the most demanding thing I have ever done in my life. It was also one of the most rewarding things I have ever done. Some of my best stories came from these travels, I hope you enjoy the stories.

TRAVELING FOR THE WHITE HOUSE

The most unique experiences I had while at The White House was the travel overseas as part of a Presidential visit. There were several distinct parts of traveling with The White House. There was the advance team, of three to six people that went several weeks ahead of the visit. The main body of support came later with over 100 people that would support the visit depending on the duration and location. Almost all the things the White House Communications Agency did for the President in the USA, we did for him on his overseas trips, but for overseas visits we had to do so much more, with more people and more equipment. In the U.S., we had the support from The White House, the local military base, the local fire department, the local police departments and more. Overseas you could not count on anything local, you had to be ready for everything with what you brought.

When you travel for The White House, you travel on diplomatic passports. We also had official passports and regular tourist passports. Depending on the mission, the location, and many other parameters depended on which passport we used. It was the first time in my life I had three active passports and I had to keep them with me at all times. You never knew when you would be called to go on a trip in the U.S. or overseas. We were given a lockable briefcase that we had to take with us with us everywhere like on vacations. The briefcase with its stuff had to stay with you at all times. If you were going away for the weekend, going on a holiday to Disney or visiting your family, you needed to take your briefcase. We kept our passports and some other classified items that we traveled with, with us all the time, so we would be ready to go whenever the call came.

Sometimes when you were on the advanced team you flew commercial. I always liked that because we got to fly first class, so you would be ready and refreshed when you arrived for a full day of work. No jet lag allowed, you hit the ground running and working.

LOGISTICS OF OVERSEAS TRAVEL

In the states, we could take a small fifteen-person team to support one event stop. This usually would only take one Air Force Cargo plane to transport the team and the equipment to the location. But, overseas we had to have about fifty or so people for the base camp (main stop) and then teams of fifteen to twenty-five people for each and every stop the President was going to make. This meant we would have to have much more equipment and that equates to more Air Force Cargo planes to transport the people and equipment. All this was just for the communications side of a visit. The Secret Service also had requirements for equipment and their vehicles, the limo, the U.S. Secret Service trail cars and other armored vehicles. Also, the Marine Helicopters most of time also came overseas, that would be more Air Force Cargo plane support. The Marine detachment would fold back the helicopter rotor blades and push the helicopter into the Air Force Cargo plane and then at the destination they would open up the rotor blades again and flight test the helicopter to be used overseas.

Loading a Road Runner vehicle on a C5 going overseas

The Air Force would attach Special Airlift Mission (SAM) numbers to any Air Force mission in support of the President. The SAM missions had priority over any other mission the Air Force was doing other than a life or safety mission. This at times meant that the aircrew you got was not too happy, that they got pulled off some other important mission to just fly around a bunch of people in civilian clothes with Top Secret equipment on a mission they knew nothing about. The SAM missions were all coordinated and set up by The White House Airlift Operations group in the Old Executive Office Building on The White House grounds. I got to know those guys pretty well. The more overseas missions you did the more coordination you had with the Airlift Operations team.

OVERSEAS GIFTS

Overseas it is very often the custom to give and receive gifts. As I became more senior as a Presidential Communications Officer and started going on overseas advances, I learned more about this part of the job. A lot of the times the embassy would take care of providing the gift that I would give to the hosting country. Sometimes The White House advance person would take care of all the gift giving and receiving. But every now and then I would find myself in a situation where it was squarely on my shoulders to be ready for this type of ceremony or event of giving and receiving gifts. I always traveled overseas with some small items that I had personally purchased, I always had some White House items with the Presidents Seal on it or some other type of Washington D.C. type item. The Military Aide would be given a handful of items from The White House for each trip for just such events. I would get some of these from the Military Aide and use these gifts as needed during the trip. These were things like tie tacks, cufflinks, paperweights and other small things with the

Presidential Seal on them and maybe the presidential signature/name.

These gifts were very sought after by The White House team too. Because we would never get anything like this and you couldn't just purchase this stuff it had to come from The White House itself to get these types of things. Sometimes you would get five White House gifts sometimes fifteen depending on the length of the trip and what country you were going to. Some country's you could get a lot more done with a gift then an official request. We never, ever bribed anyone to help or support our trips, we didn't have to, after all it was the President that was coming and that is why we were asking for things.

Cup holder and a paperweight both with POTUS sign

But sometimes things sure would move faster and we would get exactly what we wanted if we had a gift to give someone.

The same went the other way, I would receive gifts from the country we were visiting. If I gave someone a gift for helping me, I would usually get a little something in return. This was just the custom in many countries. We were supposed to turn in all gifts given to us and record them and do all this paperwork. But, if the gift was less than a certain value you didn't have to do any of that. I later found out it was very hard to determine value of some of these off the wall gifts. I would always ask the state department liaison what he thought of something and almost every time they would say don't worry about it keep that. It would take more to report it then to just let me keep it. I do have a couple of items that I was allowed to keep that have some great memories. I have one item I received from Russia and one from China from the two state visits I was the lead on towards the end of my time at The White House. I have these on my shelf in my office at home.

Sometimes I did not use up all The White House gifts that I was given form my trips. I would hand these out to my team for their outstanding work. If someone did exceptional work I would make a big deal out of giving them one of The White House gifts, in front of everyone else, at the end of the trip if I had any left. Again, we didn't get a lot of perks for working at The White House but this was one of them. I myself have some White House cufflinks with the Presidential Seal on them that I have used ever since I left The White House. I also have a White House tie tac that I still use with the Presidential symbol on it. These two items remind me all the time of the fun and the people I worked with at The White House.

PRESIDENTIAL ENVOY

As an experience Presidential Communications Officer (PCO), I started traveling on more advance trips with the advance team setting up Presidential visits. When I traveled as the senior PCO on the advanced team I was considered a "Presidential Envoy of the United States." This gives you diplomatic status that is equal to or may be one step above the U.S. Ambassador in the country your visiting. This has some unforeseen consequences that I found out about when I started travel on the advance team as the President's communications representative.

Usually the communications guy and the security folks arrive way before any White House staff person arrives. When The White House staff person arrives, they take over as the head Presidential Envoy and they get to do all the meet & greats, receptions and events. But when it is just the PCO and the Secret Service, the PCO is the top Presidential Envoy, which means I had to do all the political stuff, presenting my credentials to the head contacts in the country we were visiting. After they get your name and contact information, everyone wants to schmooze with you. They don't understand that you don't have any political clout. They just know you're the top dog from the U.S. so you get invited to all sorts of events and have to represent the President and the U.S. at these events. This is a downside because you only have so much time to get things ready for the Presidents visit. With this knowledge we would send an extra or back up senior Presidential Communications Officer to the countries you know this will be an issue. One PCO would do all the schmoozing and one would get started on the work right away.

The upside to be a Presidential Envoy is when you arrive at the airport you are treated like royalty, no customs, no waiting. There is usually someone there that meets you at the planes door and hand carries you through the airport. Usually a customs agent is waiting for you and just stamps your passport without even really looking at it. When you travel as a Presidential Envoy, you travel on a diplomatic passport. Once they hand carry you through the airport, there usually is an official reception party that also meets you at the airport and you do a lot of handshakes and exchanging of gifts. The U.S. Embassy personnel are always there to help you through the customs. You also get an interpreter, provided by the Embassy, that stays with you for the entire trip and a car and a driver from the Embassy motor pool. I was never told but I always knew that these were also my security/bodyguards.

You can get really spoiled when you get treated like this, hand carried through the airport, a car, a driver, an interpreter, and all the partying you want to do. However, we were there to do our mission getting setup for the President's visit and we were professionals.

THE SPAIN TRIP – JULY 1997

FAMILY VACTION INTERRUPTED

I was at Disneyworld in Orlando, Florida with my family on vacation, Sunday, 2 July 1997. It was the first real vacation since I took The White House job, January 1995. All of 1996 was taken up by campaign travel and I was always gone. Finally, in the summer of 1997, we were able to get away, or so I thought. The family had to get use to my new job, the hours which were very long, late night calls, always being gone, etc. But the wife and kids were doing ok dealing with my job, however I still needed to be there for them. We all knew what we had signed up for with the move to D.C. and that my work at The White House was going to be demanding.

I got my first break in July of 1997 the President was going overseas for a couple of weeks and all the teams had been assigned and I was not on any of them. My Information Technology team was finally running smoothly and I had fixed most of the items that they brought me onboard to do. It was time for a break, it was time to thank the family for all they had done to support me. Let's drive down to Florida and visit with family and go to Disney (one of our favorite places). We loaded up the car and off we went for the long drive from D.C. to Florida. This was over a twelve-hour drive but I didn't mind, I liked driving and my kids and wife slept most of the way. We visited with family in Florida and then went off for a couple of days at Disney. We had signed into the Shades of Green, military recreational hotel at Disney, had purchased multiday park hopper passes and headed off to the park. This would be a great get away, a great break – or so I thought. There we were just getting into the park on main street and my government issued White House cellphone rang! Nothing good comes of your work cellphone ringing when you're on vacation.

I answered the phone and there was The White House on the other end and the questions started. "LTC Gelhardt, are you in Orlando," I answered, "Yes." "Do you have your

White House briefcase with you," I answered "Yes." Maybe this was just a test to see if the system worked, if I followed the rules and brought my White House briefcase with my badge, and other classified items with me? I was hoping that was all this was. Then the questions continued, "Where am I in Orlando," my answer "Disney World." "Which Park", "The Magic Kingdom." I had, had enough and I asked "What is this all about." "Hold one please" was the response. I turned to my wife, who was not so happy with me and said, "Take the kids and look around main street, I will meet you in a little bit, let me see what this is all about." There went my family, wife not so happy, kids not even noticing what was going on, but I could feel all that tension that we were trying to resolve within my marriage all come flooding back.

I was waiting on hold and then finally after about five minutes they came back on and said that I was being deployed to Spain in support of the President's trip, which had changed and they needed more folks on the road. The White House Operations Center said that there would be a limo out in front of the Magic Kingdom park in fifteen minutes that would take me to my hotel and then to the airport. The plane ticket was waiting for me, so I could take a plane directly to Spain. The plane was leaving in two hours and I would have to get moving right now to make it on time and I could not miss this flight. What was I going to tell my wife and kids? My wife would have to drive back to D.C. with the kids all on their own. I knew she would not like this news and I would hear about this later. Well orders, were orders – I had to go. I told the wife and kids, and off I went to the airport and to Spain.

MY FIRST PRESIDENTIAL TRIP OVERSEAS

I arrived in the island of Majorca (also spelled Mallorca), Spain and found out that the President would be arriving the afternoon of Wednesday, 5 July 1995 and my team and I only had 36 hours to do what normally takes a week to do. The President was coming to Europe for a NATO Summit in Madrid and had added on two days and one night on the front of his trip. Spain's King Juan Carlos and Queen Sofia had invited President Clinton to vacation in Majorca with them before the NATO Summit. The President was coming to visit with the King and Queen and stay overnight at the Royal Palace of La Almudaina. The President was going to go to visit the Bellver Castle and to go out on the King's Yacht.

The part of the trip I was responsible for was the backbone communications and information technology for the President. The priority was the office we were going to set up at the palace where the President was spending the night at. He was going to stay overnight in the Royal Palace of La Almudaina, which is a historical palace of the Royal Family. The Royal Palace is a fortified palace, that was built as a Moorish castle built in the 10th century, with castle walls all around it and tall towers. The palace has a museum on the lower floors that was open to the public (closed for the President's visit of course). The top section of the palace is a modern, large apartment with several bedrooms, bathrooms, a large living room, and a kitchen.

My team and the equipment arrived and we got started working right away. The team had all been called in to meet this new mission, but we were used to doing this.

Remember, these folks were the best of the best no slackers here. We had all been on different flights and all had jetlag but that didn't matter we had work to do and we started right away. Our mission was to setup communications and computer technology for the President and the Secret Service for his visit to Majorca and for his stay overnight. I met the Facilities Manager for the palace and he introduced all his staff. Everyone was given a visitor's name tag with a White House security pin that would allow access into the secure area we would be using.

NAMETAGS ARE IMPORTANT

My team was so great, we had been working for way over twenty-four hours straight. Everyone was pulling their weight. It was about midnight or so and we were going strong. We were almost finished and the President would be coming at noon the next day. There was no sleep for anyone on the team. We would work until we were finished, right up until the last minute if that was what it took. It was dark out everyone else had already left the building and it was extremely quite in this big old castle. My guys were still pulling telephone cables and crawling under desks and behind things. I had my jacket off and my tie pulled down and I was helping. While I was under a table in the office area pulling cable, I heard someone at the door of the room. It was a little after midnight and there was a very nicely dressed man and woman standing in the door.

I got up from the floor, tightened my tie and put on my jacket that had my nametag and my White House pin on it. I introduced myself to the visitors and told them I was with The White House advanced team and we were getting the office set up for the President's visit. I apologized for making too much noise and hoped my team and I were not bothering them. This nice couple asked a few questions about what I was doing and asked about me and my team. Lastly, they asked if they could do anything for me and my team in very proper English with no Spanish accent. Then, one of the guys that was working for me that had taken my place under the table, finished pulling the cable said, "He could really use a burger, fries and a drink." All I could think was what a smartass, but I knew he was tired and we had been working nonstop. I was a little hunger too, but this is not how you asked for support. I told this nice couple we were fine and had everything we needed, that my team had been working long hours but we were almost done and would get some food and drink when we were finished. I again apologized for interrupting this nice couple and they left.

As this couple left, I was thinking to myself what was this couple doing in a secure area? They didn't introduce themselves, they didn't have any security badge, who were these people? The Secret Service had already secured the castle and were posted around the castle to ensure that the castle stayed secure. I was thinking about different scenarios of who this couple was and was thinking I should call the Secret Service and report a security breach. No one was supposed to be in this area, maybe this couple new of a secret passageway in this old castle? I was just about to call the Secret Service when I heard another person running down the hallway. I looked out the door of the room and saw the facilities manager running down the hallway putting on his jacket and dressing as he was running. This was the man I had been coordinating with, in and around the castle to get the access I needed and coordinate all the needs of The White House for these facilities.

The facilities manager came up to me and said "Please, please if you need anything I could ask him. I didn't need to ask the King and Queen!" He told me that he had woken up the kitchen staff and that there would be food in the dining room within the next fifteen minutes and that there would be food in the dining room twenty-four hours a day for the rest of our visit.

I told my folks that we would now have to send someone to the dining room to eat something for the rest of the visit. I set up a schedule with my folks, the Secret Service and some of The White House staff, so that someone would go to the dining room about every fifteen minutes for the rest of the visit. If the King and Queen told their staff to provide food, my staff would be eating it. The biggest problem was however the kitchen staff was cooking King and Queen type food, think caviar and salmon hors d'oeuvres and my guys wanted burgers and fries. Oh, well we made our bed and had to lie in it or eat it.

The moral of this story, if you meet someone in a secure area and they don't have a security nametag & pin and/or do not introduce themselves they are probably someone you should already know who they are! I had now met King Juan Carlos and Queen Sofia and almost created an international incident, so much for my first overseas visit with the President.

This was my first overseas trip and I was called off vacation to come straight to the overseas location. I was not aware that I was supposed to receive a briefing from the State Department with information about all the VIPs, to include pictures. I had never seen a picture of the King and Queen and did not know who they were. This never happened to me again, I always made sure to ask for a copy of the State Department visit packet. I would never again not be prepared.

SOMETIMES BOATS ARE NOT FUN

After the President arrived in Majorca, Spain, the King and Queen of Spain (I now knew what they looked like) invited him out on their boat for an afternoon lunch. This was an unplanned trip and we had not brought the right equipment for a boating event. As I mentioned during the campaign in 1996 we installed self-tracking, self-leveling satellite equipment in the campaign bus and train. We did not have that equipment with us and the equipment we did have with us was not easy for the end user to use when out on a boat that was bobbing around in the Mediterranean Sea.

The only solution we had to provide the instantaneous communications that we needed to provide to the President was to have one of our communications specialists on the boat with the President and the King and Queen. We went around and around with The White House staff and the Spanish protocol people to determine how to meet our mission in the boat environment. In the end the Secret Service put one person on the boat and I picked one of my communications guys to be on the boat. These two people with the communications equipment were told to go down to the forward cabin and stay in the cabin for the full trip unless there was an emergency. It was not a great ride to be in the bow of the boat bobbing up and down and not able to go outside the cabin and get some fresh air.

There were other larger Coast Guard type boats that went out to sea and were around the Kings boat to provide support if we needed it and to provide security. This was just one example of adjusting on the fly, my people could adjust and do about anything.

I talked to my guy when he got off the boat at the end of the trip and he told me he was absolutely miserable, it was hot, noisy, cramped and he did not have fun. Luckily, we did not have to set up any communications for the President during that boat trip but we were ready to meet our mission.

MY PHONE KEEP'S RINGING

After the President and First Lady went out on the boat with the King and Queen of Spain, they participated in couple of other events that day and finally came to the Royal Palace of La Almudaina for their overnight stay. It had been an extremely long day for most of my team and for myself. Finally, we could all get a couple of hours of sleep. I decided to send my team back to the hotel that was about a mile or two away from the palace. There weren't any real places for my team to sleep at the palace. The palace really only had the apartment that the President and First Lady and some staffers were staying in and the facilities managers apartment. I decided to stay at the palace and got an Army cot so I could sleep onsite with the President. As explained in Chapter 5, four folks have to be with the President at all times and since I was the PCO for this period I had to be there. I got my cot and set it up next to the telephone equipment that we had put into the palace down in the basement of the tower. We had strung telephone wire from the microwave relay tower that we put on the tower/roof, down the circular stairs to the basement mobile telephone switch that we traveled with and then we ran cable off that switch up to the different places that needed phones. Like the overnight apartment that the President and First Lady were staying in. Also, we ran cables and phones to each one of the Secret Service guard posts and to the office space we setup for the President.

We often traveled with mobile telephone switches and microwave relay towers and many other items, some of which were classified equipment. This allowed us to setup telephones were ever they were needed and make them act just like they did at The White House. The Secret Service and the President could pick up the phone and dial numbers just like they were back in the United States at The White House. It made it really easy on them this way. We would encrypt the phone call and then microwave the call from one location to our local base of operations locations. We would have everything come into a central telephone hub and then tie it back to the U.S. through the local telephone network. The folks in the U.S. would unencrypt the call and then send it over the local landlines to the person that was being calling.

It was about midnight and I was exhausted. I made my rounds to the Secret Service posts to made sure everyone had radio and phone communications or whatever they needed. Everything was good, all the equipment was working and I was beat. I had had maybe three hours of sleep in the last two days since I got on the ground. It seemed to me that this location was a job well done and it was time for me to get some rest. The President would be leaving early the next morning and my job was almost done. I went down to my cot and passed out.

The next morning, I got up around 5:00 AM and started making my rounds to make sure everything was ok. I first checked with the Secret Service posts on the morning shift to make sure they had communications and it was up and running with no issues. I had time to check the two-primary guard post and found that the day shift reported that there was some type of phone problem overnight? I asked them what was the problem and they said they did not know. Both guard post had the phones unplugged. I plugged in both the phones and did test calls back to The White House switch board and both phones worked just fine. I asked the Secret Service agent to test the phones and make sure they worked and they did. So, I just let it go as a non-issue that I would have to investigate more later.

The President was going to leave at 6:00 AM, so after I checked with the two primary guard posts, I had to go out and make sure the motorcade was all setup. As I mentioned earlier my team was responsible for the communications for the motorcade. I always came behind my team and double checked that things were getting done. Of course, my team was on top of it, everything with the motorcade was great.

The President left the Royal Palace of La Almudaina on time and headed off to Air Force One to leave the island of Majorca. When the President left I had to do my standard security sweep of the Presidential area before I could release the Secret Service and before my guys could start breaking down our equipment. When I made it up to the apartment that the President and First Lady used to stay overnight. I noticed that all the telephones that my team had put in were unplugged, just like the phones at the guard post. I started to think that there was a much bigger problem with the communication and that I would need to investigate. I asked one of the staff people that stayed up in the apartment with the first family and she said that all the phones rang, on and off, all night for no good reason. She would answer the phone and no one would be on the other end. This happened to many times so she just unplugged her phone and heard the First Family's phone doing the same thing so she unplugged all the phones in the apartment area. She knew if anyone needed them that that there were other ways to communicate with them. She also told me that the President was not too happy about the phones and that they were continuing to ring for no reason. I told my team we could not break down our equipment until we figured out what the problem was. We had to trouble shoot the issue that happened during the night, with the phones ringing. I know that I would have an explain to most likely the President what the issue was. We tested all our equipment and it worked just fine. We could not find any issue? I was up on the tower of the palace right next to the microwave tower that we installed and was with one of my communications specialist testing the equipment and could not find any issues with that equipment.

As we were checking our equipment on the tower I looked over to the airfield. You could see the airfield very well from the tower of the palace. I heard Air Force One getting ready for takeoff. The airfield was off to the east of town and the palace. As I watch Air Force One take off, I notice that the flight path for the takeoffs this morning was east to west. I watch Air Force One roll down the runway and takeoff. I could see Air Force One climbed into the sky and turned over the city to the ocean. It was amazing to see the plane so close to were I was standing and right as Air Force One passed the palace, guess what happened? The microwave tower we were using lost communication to the second tower across the city that we had the line of sight too. After Air Force One passed between the two towers breaking the microwave connection. The towers reconnected after the plane passed and did a self-test cycle to make sure everything worked. Well when this equipment does a self-test, it sends power down the phone lines to check the lines and that makes all the phones on the line ring. As Air Force One went by I heard over my radio several people ask what we had just done because the phones all rang and there was no one on the line. Well we had not done anything other then watch Air Force One fly by.

Microwave equipment on top of the Palace

We waited for a second plane to take off from the airport the same thing happened and I knew we had found the issue. I made some calls and found out that the airport had changed their take off and landing directions during the night. On the previously days when we were setting up our equipment, the landing and takeoff directions was from west to east. During the night the winds had shifted and the airport had changed take off and landing directions from west to east to east to west. Because of this change every plane that took off flew right through our microwave shot from the palace to the hotel that we were using as our base of operations. Every time the airplane broke the microwave link the system did a self-test when it reconnected and rang all the phones.

Now I had the answer to the issue. I knew I was going to get yelled at but I had call Air Force One and tell my boss about the issue. I called Air Force One and asked for my boss who was traveling with the President on the plane. When he got on the phone he told me that the President had already yelled at him for providing poor telephone service. He already knew the phones rang all night long. The President had told him that information when they talked. Luckily the President was in a good mood and this issue just got dropped.

I added a new knowledge base issue to the use of the microwave towers. Now air travel lanes are part of the planning when setting up this type of equipment. I left my mark in the training books, got a great story out of this event, and didn't get fired. I would say that was a win!

THE ARGENTINA TRIP – OCT 1997

BUTCH AND SUNDANCE

The President was going to Argentina to meet with President Menem of Argentina. I was on the advance team as the Presidential Communications Officer for the San Carlos de Bariloche location and went down several weeks early. As part of the advance team for the trip, The White

House staff was developing a full agenda of what the President would be doing while on the ground. When the staff was looking at event locations around town they would ask the Secret Service and the communications folks to come along and provide input for those locations.

So, in the weeks leading up to the President's visit the staff guy, the interpreter, the Secret Service guy and myself were all around town. The locals got to know who we were, it was a small town. Well one day, we had been looking at event locations all morning and wanted to take a break to eat lunch. We asked our interpreter if he knew of a local place where we could get something to eat. He said he knew of a really great restaurant that served all kinds of meat off the grill but it was a little bit out of town, in the middle of no were. We had, had a full morning and thought why not let's see some of the countryside and take a long lunch.

President arrival in Argentina – Military Honor Guard

The interpreter, who was also our driver provided by the U.S. Embassy in Argentina, started driving out of town until we got to an old wooden cabin with a wood barn behind it and cattle out in the fields around it. It looked like a farm in a beautiful setting, cattle, sheep, pigs, with a really nice river next to the grounds. It did not look like a restaurant and we wondered if the interpreter misunderstood what we had been talking about. We got out of the car and noticed several other cars in front of the farmhouse cabin and noticed the grounds in front of this place could hold a lot of cars.

We opened the door, walked in and found a very cozy restaurant with a firepit in the middle of the building with an open flame and a movable rack on chains that could be lifted up or lowered down. The rack had some meat on it and you could see the cook standing there tending to what he was cooking over the open flame. The place had the smell of beef cooking in the air – it smelled great.

At the airport with Air Force One in Argentina

As soon as we came in the door, everyone (they all seemed to be locals) in the restaurant stopped talking and turned to see the foreigners walking in the door. A man came running up to us and started shaking our hands and led us to a table right next to the firepit in the middle of the restaurant. He was talking so fast our interpreter was having a very hard time interpreting at the same speed. We later found out that this man was the owner of the restaurant and knew we were the "White House Team" that had been around the area looking for places for the President to go. He thought we were here to check out his restaurant for the President of the United States to eat there.

He started talking to all his staff and they all got to work. We didn't even have a chance order anything off the menu or even look at a menu. We found out through the interpreter that the owner ordered one of everything on the menu for us, that our meal was on him and he wanted us to taste everything they served. We did in fact taste everything he put on the table. It was the most fantastic beef, pork, lamp I have ever eaten. The cook would move the grill rack up and down over the fire depending on what he was cooking and we could see everything. It was like sitting in your kitchen at home smelling the smells and seeing the work.

As the food was cooking, the owner showed us around the old farmhouse and the barn area. He was so proud of his place and explained the history of the farm to us. He showed us a couple of very old newspapers article with black and white photos in them – that showed outlaws Robert LeRoy Parker (Butch Cassidy) and Harry Longabaugh (the Sundance Kid) in the photo. He explained that when Butch Cassidy and the Sundance Kid left the U.S. they came down to Argentina and lived in this area for a while. They built the farmhouse and the barn and had a business of taking people across the river next to the farm. They had a river crossing barge and charged people to cross. They also opened up a small restaurant for travelers that were passing by. But farming and the straight life was not for them and they returned to a life of crime in South America, were they were killed in Bolivia.

It was a very good restaurant for meat, and had the local flavor. Even though we were not looking for this place for the President, he ended up going there for a meal while in the Bariloche area. This restaurant had the best beef I have ever tasted in my life. We would eat their several times while on this trip when we had a break from work.

HORSEBACK RIDING

President Clinton and President Menem meet at the Llao hotel complex outside of the city of San Carlos de Bariloche in Argentina. This was a nice resort area in the mountains, with a golf course (so the HMX1 Marine Helicopters could land there). The first day when President Clinton meet with the President of Argentina, he was presented a horse as a gift. Then the whole schedule got turned upside down by the Argentina President, when he indicated he would like to go horseback riding with President Clinton the next day.

The great schedule The White House advance team had made for the President were scrapped and redone to include a horse riding event the next day. This happened to the President's schedule all the time, we always had to adjust to what the President wanted to do. That night the Secret Service and The White House staff were trying to figure out what we were going to do, how would we provide security and communications during a horseback riding trip up into the mountains around the resort. Well, the ride was going to happen and we had to support it. I asked my team, "Did anyone ride." I was trying to find my options and see what we could do. Out of everyone on my team I was the only one that had medium to advanced riding skills. I was picked to ride along with the two Presidents and take my communications equipment with me on a pack horse. The Secret Service also did the same thing. They picked out of their ranks folks that could ride and we all went riding up the mountain with the two Presidents the next day.

I had followed the President in a golf cart before and traveled with him in a boat, now I was following him around on a horse, that was a first. But my team and I could adjust to just about anything. We made sure we could still meet the mission even on horseback.

THE SENEGAL, AFRICA TRIP - APRIL 1998

DAKAR AIRPORT

President Clinton was finishing the last leg of a six-nation tour of Africa. The President had several stops to include; a visit with the President of Senegal at his Presidential Palace in Dakar, a military base used to train Senegalese troops as a U.S. backed African peacekeeping forces, a visit to a village rejuvenated by U.S. Aid, and lastly Slave Island off the coast of Senegal. The home base for this trip was going to be the city of Dakar, the Capital of the country of Senegal, on the West Coast of Africa. Senegal has been a democracy since its independence in 1960 and has been a stabilizing force/country in Africa.

My team landed in a U.S. Air Force Cargo plane, at the Dakar airfield about two weeks ahead of the visit to get things setup. I was absolutely amazed at the width and length of the runway when we landed on. This was the widest runway I have ever landed on (four times as wide as a normal commercial runway) and when we got out of the plane I noticed it was one of the longest runways I had ever seen (it had to be over three miles long). I could not even see the end of the runway. This became doubly amazing when we pulled up to a very old open air one story terminal building. The tallest building around on the airport was a small three-story tower building attached to the terminal that looked like it was from the beginning of the age of flight. I think the tail of our plane was higher than the tower building.

I had to ask the folks at the airport why the runway was so large? It turned out that the Dakar airport was a Transoceanic Abort Landing (TAL) site for the NASA space shuttle program. NASA paid to build this very long and very wide runway on the western tip of Africa at the beginning of the Space Shuttle program in the early 1970s as an alternate landing site for the shuttle. Dakar was given the runway for their use and was supposed to keep up the runway over time. As a side note, in 1987 NASA replaced the Dakar runway as a TAL site due to unsatisfactory conditions and deficiencies. Even though everything at the airport looked old and run down the runway was in good enough condition for Air Force One to land for our visit, or so I was told later.

As we tried to offload our equipment off the Air Force transport plane that brought us to Dakar, we found that this airport did not have the necessary equipment to accomplish this mission. We were going to have to unload the whole plane by hand and then reload trucks to just unload again when we got to the hotel. But, our advance guy, that had arrived a couple of days ahead of us, showed up with a large forklift and a flatbed semi-truck. We offloaded our equipment, that was tied down on the Air Force pallets, in the cargo plane right onto the flatbed truck. Since our equipment was Top Secret stuff, we had a car drive in front of the flatbed truck and a car drive behind the flatbed truck to provide security just in case anything may fallen off – which it didn't.

The hotel was only about a mile away from the airport so we only had to go back and forth with the truck and the forklift four or five times. But that was better than unloading and reloading all our equipment by hand.

Our Hotel was a walled in compound with gate guards and guard towers around the hotel all the way down to the beach area. It felt like we were in a prison each time we went into and came out of the compound. But inside the compound there was a four or five-star resort hotel complete with a great beach. We used the forklift that followed us down the street from the airport to unload the flatbed truck and then started to setup our equipment. Getting ready for our next adventure here in Africa.

MILITARY BASE

The President went out to a military air base west of the capital, basically in the middle of the desert, of Senegal, to review the training of troops of the African Peacekeeping Force. It was a real eye opener for me, I am a military member of the greatest Army in the world, the U.S. Army. I have been deployed to the desert, to combat, to the field for training, and much more. But what I saw at this African base just amazed me, because of everything they did not have. They did not have the equipment and facilities, that I am so used to in the U.S. Military. I had more equipment and support when I deployed to the field then these troops had at their home military base.

How can anyone be effective as a fighting force without the proper equipment and support of your chain of command. But I could tell they had the right heart. They put on a demonstration of training and used what they had and did a great job.

I have always felt proud to be part of the U.S. Army but like anyone else I have complained at times for not having what I thought I needed. Now I felt bad about all those times I have complained about not having the right equipment. These guys had next to nothing and they were out there trying hard, and doing great, good for them.

AFRICA VILLAGE

We flew from the military base out to the middle of nowhere and landed in a big open field of dirt. The pre-site survey done by the helicopter folks, told us that this landing area was a dust hazard, but they could make it happen.

I told you in a previous chapter about the ground stop procedure used when Air Force One moves all the other air planes have to stay still. This same type of system is used when the Presidents helicopter moves all other helicopters are supposed to be still. But, because of the condition of the landing site all the helicopters came in a formation and all landed at the same time. Because after the first helicopter came in and started kicking up dust you couldn't see anything.

I was on the ground when the helicopters landed

The helicopters landed and kicked up so much dust that we had to wait several minutes before we could open the doors to the helicopters to get out. It looked like there was one dirt path in and out of this village, no paved road, no power, no anything. There was no motorcade, we all just started walking to the village that was about half a mile away. The village was just a cluster of huts with one more substantial cement block type building that was the schoolhouse & clinic that the U.S. helped build.

The people at this village were so incredibly friendly and nice. They were so thankful for the school/clinic but they were more thankful for the fresh drinking water that they now had out of a brand new well that was built with the help of the U.S. They had never had fresh water in their village before to drink and farm with. I just can't image that type of life, these people had, they had nothing but also had everything – friendly, nice, smiling, helpful, great family and community groups. A little bit of aid not as a hand out, but a hand up, to help them up was amazing.

SLAVE ISLAND OF DAKAR

The White House wanted to go out to the island of "Ile De Goree" or as it is better known "Slave Island." Goree is a small island that is 3,000 feet in length and 1150 feet in width, sheltered by the Cap-Vert Peninsula. It is a short ferry ride from the mainland harbor of Dakar. The island of Goree was one of the first places in Africa to be settled by Europeans, as the Portuguese settled on the island in 1444.

Goree is known as the location of the Maison des Esclaves, or Slave House, built by an Afro-French family about 1780-1784. The Slave House is one of the oldest houses on the island. It is the home of the infamous "Door of No Return" which is said to be the last place exported slaves touched African soil for the rest of their lives.

We toured this small island and went to the Slave House. The front of the house looked like a normal large mansion, but when you go into the basement area, there were cage areas for slaves. There was also a door off the back of the house that lead out to a dock were transatlantic slave ships could pull right up to, for loading. Slaves would be taken out of the cages and out that back door right onto ships to take them across the Atlantic to the Americas.

I handled the visit to Slave Island, setting up all the communications and support for the President's visit. On the island I got to meet Jesse Jackson who was traveling with the President on his six-nation tour of Africa. The visit to the island was a major press event with more press on the island then locals. It was educational to see this part of history and learn more about the whole system of slavery. I would have never seen this place and learned what I did if it wasn't for this Presidential trip.

THE GERMANY TRIP – MAY 1998 50th ANNIVERSARY OF THE BERLIN AIRLIFT

One of the great things about working at The White House was it gave me the occasion to be at historic events, to re-learn history, to live right in the middle of new history, and to meet historic people like Pilot Gail Halvorsen. I am so thankful for all those people before us that laid down the foundation for what we have today.

President Clinton and Chancellor Helmut Kohl both participated in the 50th Anniversary of the Berlin Airlift at the Tempelhof Airport, in Berlin, Germany. The event marked the 50th anniversary of the Berlin Airlift, the historic effort to defeat the Soviet blockade of the city of Berlin. The Berlin Airlift was the first large-scale, peacetime use of airlift in executing national policy and was called the first battlefield of the Cold War. The first missions were flown to Berlin on June 26, 1948, airlifting 4.4 billion tons of milk, flour, medicine, fuel and other cargo over a fifteen-month period ending in May 1949.

As part of the ceremony, President Clinton dedicated a brand-new U.S. Air Force, Boeing C-17 cargo plane. This was the first time I had seen the Air Forces new C-17 plane up close. I was able to take a tour of it and it was simply amazing, especially when you put it next to the old Air Force, Douglas C-47 used during the Berlin Airlift. The old C-47 planes landed every three to four minutes twenty-four hours a day, seven days a week, providing supplies needed to keep Berlin going. It's amazing how our tools and technology have changed so much, the new C-17 holds the same amount of cargo (about 80 tons) on one trip as one C-47 took on 32 trips.

The President and Chancellor Kohl both gave speeches and reviewed a formation of military troops. The best part of the Presidents ceremony was to dedicate this new C-17 and reveal the name painted on its side "The Spirit of Berlin" and introducing Pilot Gail Halvorsen.

I was able to meet Gail Halvorsen, a U.S. Air Force pilot who became known by grateful Germans as "The Candy Bomber" for his unauthorized airdrops of sweets via mini-parachutes over the end of the runway. It was an honor to meet him and several other World War II pilots that participated in this historic event and shake their hands.

I remember several years ago when East and West of Germany were still divided I was stationed in Germany with the Army. Every military member coming and going from Germany went through Rhein-Main Air Force Base across from the civilian airport in Frankfurt. When at Rhein-Main you could not miss the large memorial at the front gate that had a plaque on it talking about the Berlin Airlift and showed three large arcs' up in the air pointing towards Berlin. When I was at Tempelhof Airfield (in a now consolidated Germany) I was able to see the other co-memorial of the one I saw in Rhein-Main. It also has three large arcs' up in the air pointing towards the three main airfields used to supply Berlin, of which Rhein-Main Air Force Base was one of those bases. I wonder if the other two bases in Germany also have a similar memorial?

STONE 1745

On President Clinton's two-day visit to Germany, one of his stops was a bilateral discussion with Chancellor Kohl at the Sanssouci Palace, in Potsdam, Germany right outside of Berlin, Germany. I was the lead Presidential Communications Officer (PCO) for this location and the President's visit. My team and I arrived a couple of weeks before the President to setup his communications for his visit at both the Tempelhof Airport event and the event at the Sanssouci Palace. I knew no history or background of the Sanssouci Palace, this was just another fancy building the President was having an event at.

As stated in this book, my team setup and tore down our equipment over and over and over again. When The White House goes to visit somewhere we need room for the security, the staff and the communications equipment. This stop at the Sanssouci Palace was no different. My team and I didn't waste any time when we got on the ground, we started coordinating our needs with the director of the Palace. We told him what The White House needs were and what our team needs were.

One of our needs was to find a high enough location for our communications equipment. We usually go up on the roof of the highest building around and attached our antennas on whatever we can find on the roof. The director of the Palace took us up to the current roof and started looking around for a place to attach our equipment. We tried very hard not to drill holes or make any marks on historic sites like this Palace. We looked all over this roof to find something we could zip/tie, or duct tape our antenna poles to, but we could not find anything that would meet our needs. Then we started looking for the second-best thing something we could attach our antennas to with bolts. We found a stone block that had a number on it "1745", this block was standing alone and was outside some of the other roof lines that we saw. We didn't think this stone was any different than many other old buildings we had been to. It is very common for old buildings to mark or number its stones and wood pieces, so during restoration they can be taken down cleaned/fixed or whatever and then they know exactly where to put the piece back into.

We ask the director of the Palace who had the curator with him if we could attach our antenna to this block with the number "1745" on it by drilling some holes and putting bolts into it. The curator of the Palace almost had a heart attack when we asked this question. Then we were told that this was the original corner stone used in constructing the palace. The number 1745 was the date that, this last stone was put in place for the completion of the palaces first wall.

I later did some research on the Sanssouci palace and found out it was constructed between 1745-1747 for Fredrick the Great, King of Prussia as a private residence where he could relax away from the pomp and ceremony of the Berlin court. The palace's name is a French phrase (sans souci), which translates as "Without concerns" or "Carefree." I didn't know all this information while I was standing on the roof asking to drill into a two hundred and fifty-year-old historic stone. Needless to say, we did not use that stone to attach our antenna and found something else that would meet our needs.

Going overseas always reminds me how young America is. Here in Germany they were building palaces in 1745-1747 while the United States of America was a British colony and would not be a country of its own for another thirty years.

THE BATHROOM

While at the Sanssouci Palace, in Potsdam, Germany; during the bilateral discussions between President Clinton and Chancellor Kohl, there was a several hours long closed-door meeting between the two leaders. During this time, all the staff and support personnel went off in their own directions to do whatever they do. I had to stay right next to the door of the meeting room and be available just in case some type of communications was needed, a phone call, a fax, or whatever.

I was the only one standing right outside the room in the hallway, even the Secret Service was down the hallway some. When right then Chancellor Kohl stepped out of the room by his self, no security, no interpreter – just the Chancellor. When he saw me, he asked me in German where the bathroom (or in German "Badezimer") was. Well in my best German, I told him it was down the hallway and to the left (or in German "Den Flur nach links").

While in the Army I was stationed in German (1987-1991) and had picked up quite a bit of German. I used to be able to speak German at a moderate level back then but have since lost most of that ability today. But the few words and sentences I used was enough to get the job done.

I have met a lot of people while at The White House, celebrities, kings and queens, and quite a few heads of state. But this was a first for me, a one on one discussion with a foreign head of state, even if it was over the bathroom. I walked Chancellor Kohl down the hallway and showed him the way to the bathroom. On the way back from the bathroom, he thanked me and shook my hand, and started talking to me in German. I didn't have the heart to tell him I only understood about half of what he said, my German was just not that good anymore. But I did understand enough that I was able to reply a couple of times in German. I wish I could have understood the whole conversation, but a least I did not feel like a fool and I helped out a head of state.

THE BEIJING, CHINA TRIP – JUNE 1998

C-5 (SEE FIVE)

The next trip I was sent on was to China. Because this was China, there were some very serious concerns about electronic ease dropping and spying. We had to bring more equipment then we normally did on overseas trips, almost doubling our load of equipment.

Instead of flying the U.S. Air Force, C-141 Starlifter cargo aircraft, which was our normal overseas cargo plane, this time we were flying the largest military transport the U.S. Air Force had, the C-5 Galaxy. This cargo plane not only had the cargo and lift capacity we needed for our equipment but it also had an upper flight deck that could handle 73 passengers in much better comfort then the C-141. We thought the trip would be a much better ride for us since we would be sitting in regular seats with a galley and bathrooms – we were wrong.

As part of our flight plan, we left Andrews Air Force Base, in D.C. and went to an Air Force base in Alaska to refuel in route to China. My folks and I had to get off the plane during the refueling operations. Because of all the classified equipment we had on the plane, we all decided to just wait there on the tarmac and watch the refueling. After the refueling we got back on the C-5, that we arrived in, and got ready to go again. The pilot told us that during the pre-flight checks they found some maintenance issues that needed to be fixed.

Luckily, our White House support airlift missions were considered Special Assignment Air Missions (SAAM) called Phoenix Banner missions. This gave us an extremely high priority of any airlift in the Air Force. That also meant that the Air Force was ready for this type of event and had a second C-5 on the tarmac as a backup plane for our mission. We started the process of off-loading our equipment from the C-5 that brought us to Alaska and reloading the equipment onto the second C-5, that took over an hour. We all loaded on the second C-5 and got ready to go.

During the pre-flight of the second C-5, the flight team found out it was also broken and could not takeoff without being fixed. The Air Force then diverted another C-5 that was in the Alaska area and it landed at our Air Force base. It showed up full of cargo that needed to be off loaded off that plane. Then we needed to take our cargo off the second C-5 and upload it on the third C-5. During the preflight of the third C-5 – can you guess what happened?

Yes – you're right, the third C-5 also had mechanical issues and could not takeoff without some maintenance issues being reviewed. The Air Force called yet another C-5 to be diverted to our mission and it was now inbound to Alaska.

It was almost comical at this point, we had been on the tarmac for over seven hours by this time, with no food, water, or bathroom breaks. Well, after over seven hours they had fixed the first C-5 that we had come on and yes, we unloaded and reloaded our equipment again back to the original C-5. It was dark out by then and we were all very tired, but my team did a complete inventory of our equipment, were very professional and just kept on mission.

The joke that came from this trip was "Do you know why they call these planes C-5? Because you have to SEE FIVE of them before you get to where you want to go!"

On the trip home from China, I told The White House Airlift Officer that I did not want to land in Alaska for refueling and instead I wanted to air refuel over Alaska and only land in D.C. The C-5 like many other military aircraft can refuel while flying by hooking up to a KC-135 air refueling tanker plane. I did not, however, realize just how bumpy it was to refuel on a large cargo plane. It was like riding a roller coaster for over thirty minutes. It made almost all of my team sick, but at least we made it straight home, without seeing five more planes.

FORBIDDEN CITY AND THE DRAGON THRONE

I arrived in Beijing over six weeks before the Presidents arrival, this time The White House sent an official Presidential Envoy with the advance party. The envoy did all the political stuff, the parties, the meet and greets, etc.

But as a team, the whole advance party went around with the Presidential Envoy and our Chinese counterparts to visit all the locations that the president was going to visit.

One of the places we went to was the Forbidden City, which is the former Imperial Palace complex from the Ming dynasty (1420-1912), in the historic center of Beijing. The Forbidden City served as the home of the emperors and their households, as well as, the ceremonial and political center of Chinese government for almost 500 years. The complex consists of 980 buildings and covers 180 acres.

This place was impressive! We met with the curator of the of the National Palace Museum at the front gate. They had closed down the whole palace just for us, no tourist, no one walking around, just our group lead by the head of the museum, it was awesome! We had a firsthand tour and the curator showed us all the back rooms and areas that the normal tourist did not see.

When we got to the largest of the main three halls, the "Hall of Supreme Harmony" the curator took down the barrier in front of the throne and we walked right up to it. He was telling us all about the history of the term "Dragon Throne" and how it was used to identify the throne of the Emperor of China and its significances in Chinese history. Then he unexpectedly asked if the Presidential Envoy would like to sit on this historic throne. We all looked at the Presidential Envoy and he did not move towards the throne.

I was the closest one to the throne, so the Envoy looked at me and gave me a head nod. I walked over and sat on this many hundred-year-old Imperial Dragon Throne. This was a thrill for me to be able to touch such an old piece of history, not understanding what had just happened politically.

I later found out how a picture of the Presidential Envoy sitting on the Emperors throne would have been very bad press for The White House. Since, no one really knew who I was a picture of a nobody like me on the throne was a none event, with no press value. At the same time that the Chinese were doing political maneuvering before the Presidential visit the U.S. was maneuvering right back by putting a commoner, like me, on the throne. No picture was taken of me on the throne, to bad I would have like to have one!

RUNNING THE WALL

We had gone to the Great Wall of China for an official visit to review that site for the Presidential visit. The area of the wall we went to was in very good condition and had been kept up for the tourists and this is where the President would come. The Great Wall of China is a site to see and I highly recommend anyone that is traveling to this part of the world go see it.

During the advance period, while we were setting up our equipment and getting ready for the President to arrive, we tried to do some tourist stuff when we had time. We found some time to be on our own and went back to the wall. Several of us brought our running gear just in case we could find time to run the Great Wall of China. It was fantastic to run up and down the hills of the Great Wall of China.

We started where the wall was in good condition and ran several miles until we got to a point in the wall that had not been kept up. The wall was still amazing even in this area where it needed a lot of repair. Parts of the wall had decayed over time and was crumbling down. Nature had taken over this portion of the wall, the decay was due to vines and trees growing out of the side and the middle of the wall. As you looked further down the wall as far as the eyes could see, the wall was in decay, time had taken its toll. But even with all the decay and plant life you could tell where the wall was and the size of it.

We ran back to the area were the tourists were and where the wall was in good condition. I can't believe we ran the wall, it was a lot of fun, it was a bucket list item and I was fortunate enough to be able to check it off my list. We worked very hard supporting the President and The White House, but we also found some times to play hard and check things off our bucket list!

SHRIMP MAN

One night a group of us went out to get a local Chines dinner. There were several Secret Service guys that went out with my team. We asked at the front desk of our hotel were to go to get some good local food. We walked down the street to a local place that was recommended.

We were all ordering different types of food. Some of our group, were not too sure of what they ordered, but we were all exploring the local culture and the local food. One of the Secret Service agents ordered fresh shrimp as his meal. This Secure Service guy was a big man, he was 6'4" tall, weighing over 250lbs and was all muscle.

We were all receiving our food and seeing what we were getting as several of us didn't really know what we ordered.

The Secret Service agent that ordered the fresh shrimp or so he thought, had a hot plate put in front of him. Then they brought out a big pot of boiling water that they put on top of the hot plate, then they put an empty plate in front of him and a covered bowl next to him. Then a server came out and picked up the covered bowl and took off the cover and dumped live shrimp into the boiling pot of water. They had not put the lid, on the pot of boiling water, fast enough. The live shrimp were jumping out of the pot of boiling water as fast as they could. Since the pot was right in front of the big tough Secret Service agent all the shrimp were jumping out right into his face and body.

You never saw a big guy move so fast, he knocked down his chair and knocked over the whole table with all the food on it. Everything and everybody was falling everywhere. The pot of boiling shrimp fell over and the shrimp were jumping all over everything, along with all the other food that was now on the floor and all over all of us. This scene reminded me of a three stooges movie, everyone was laughing and rolling on the floor with food everywhere.

We never did get any food to eat that night. We were asked to leave the restaurant, which we did. We made the big Secret Service agent that caused all this havoc pay for everyone's meals, that we didn't get to eat. We never let the agent forget this adventure. His new nickname on the radio now was "Shrimp Man" and that nickname followed him around even after this trip.

BEIJING VISIT

President Clinton, Secretary of State Madeleine Albright, along with several congressmen and cabinet members came to China for an eight-day visit to three locations. I was responsible for all the communications and technology for all the sites for the three-days that they would be in the Beijing area. This was the biggest responsibility I had received since working at The White House.

Chinese flip phone given to us as gifts.

I was one of the most experience Presidential Communications Officers (PCO) by this time and I felt like The White House had a lot of confidence in my ability to keep The White House communications secure in this environment. This was one of the most technical trips with the most security risks that I had been on. I wish I could write more about what we did and how we did it, but I believe those tools and techniques used back then would still be considered classified even today.

Let me give you one small example of the security challenges of this trip. The whole advanced party was provided free flip phones, from the Chinese government, to use during our visit. The flip phones where imprinted with "President Clinton visit to China" and the dates of the visit.

We all knew we could not use these phones because we knew they would all be monitored by the Chinese government. I still have my free flip phone sitting on my bookcase at home.

THE MOSCOW, RUSSIA TRIP - SEPTEMBER 1998

THE KREMLIN

I did so well on the China trip that The White House ask for me by name to handle the Moscow, Russia trip. This trip to Russia was a two-day summit between President Clinton and Russian President Boris Yeltsin. Just like China, we arrived six weeks early to set things up prior to the President's visit. Again, this time The White House sent an official Presidential Envoy with the advanced team. This trip to Russia was a lot easier than our trip to China. There were fewer locations that the President was going to visit. It was really a working trip all around the Kremlin complex of buildings and his meetings there.

Most people have heard of the Kremlin but don't understand that it is a large fortified complex in the heart of Moscow, with Red Square right outside of it to it's east. The word "Kremlin" means "Fortress inside a city" and is often used to refer to the government of Russia similar to how the "White House" is used to refer to the government of the U.S.

The Kremlin site has been continuously inhabited since the 2nd century BC. The current Kremlin and its walls were built between 1485-1495 and replaced a white limestone walled complex that was built over a hundred years earlier in the 1300's. The part of this complex, that we went, to was the Grand Kremlin Palace built between 1837-1849. The Grand Palace complex serves as the official residence of the President of Russia, like The White House does for the U.S. President.

When we went to the Grand Kremlin Palace for the first time I was very surprised to meet with President Boris Yeltsin. He met with the whole advance White House team and talked with each one of us, shook our hands and gave us each a gift from the Kremlin. I was able to keep the gift I received from President Yeltsin and still have it on my bookshelf at home. It is a beautiful metal with gold leaf rendering of the Kremlin that came in a nice wooden box.

The gift from President Yeltsin

MOTORCADE:

During the President's two-day visit to Russia there was a lot of coordination that needed to be handled by The White

House. The meeting locations, events list, topics to discuss and more. All these issues are what I see as political juggling and the Presidential Envoy took care of resolving these things.

There was one issue that I had to handle that put me in the middle of what could have been an international crisis. The Secret Service had coordinated all the security issues around the President's visit with the Russian security people at the Kremlin, to include how we managed our Presidential motorcade. We had explained in advance the size of the motorcade and what we would need from the local security folks to meet our security needs. But the first time the full motorcade was assembled was at the Vnukovo Airport waiting for the President to arrive on Air Force One.

It was about two hours before Air Force One was due to land and we had the full motorcade lined up and ready to go. I was checking with the Senior Secret Service agent on the ground and told him the full motorcade was ready to go. At that time, we were both asked to meet with the local Chief of Police on the tarmac. We went over to talk to him and were told that the motorcade was too long, that we had to cut the motorcade in half. Here we were on the tarmac waiting for the President to arrive and they wanted us to change everything. There were some very big security and communications issues with splitting up the motorcade. I took the lead in this discussion and told the Chief of Police that we would not split the motorcade, that we had permission for the motorcade the way it was. The Chief called over a high ranking military person and talked to that person and then turned to us and said, "No, you must split the motorcade and that is final." This was getting out of hand, so I told them that I would have to call Air Force One and talk to them on this topic. I called over one of my guys and he handed me a secure satellite phone. I asked the Chief and the military guy one more time if his word was final. This poor guy was now sweating and looked very uncomfortable. He turned to the military guy, who at this time also looked nervous and he said this was his final word.

I called Air Force One and asked for my boss on Airforce one using code names. But, I told the interpreter that I was talking to the President at that time. I told the interpreter that the President of the United States wanted to know what was going on. I told the interpreter that if Russia could not meet the needs of the President and allow all of his staff and press to be in his motorcade he would just turn around and not come to Russia.

By the time the interpreter told the Chief of Police what I was say, this guy's eyes were darting all over and he was sweating more. Finally, the military guy next to him looked over to a black limo at the side of the airport. You could tell these two were nervous and they were not in control. They were just doing what someone told them to do. Finally, a man in a black suit standing over by the black limo shook his head and the Chief said everything was just fine with the motorcade.

I turned to the satellite phone told my boss (not the President) what was going on and that everything was just fine. More politics and political juggling by the Russians.

CHAPTER 10
Outstanding Military Support

The men and women that are in the Military and have volunteered to serve their country are an unquiet set of individuals. Less than one percent of the U.S. population serve in the military and protect our country. The military members I served with at The White House, were the best of the best. You will never find a more dedicated, flag waving group of folks in your life.

An old saying goes – "A leader is not a leader if no one follows." I am humbled by the young men and women that have allowed me to lead them. I am very proud of my time in the Army, in the Military, and at The White House.

PRESIDENTIAL EVENT ON BASE

I loved doing events at military bases, you show up with your White House credentials and everyone on that base bends over backward for anything you want or need from the Base Commander on down. I was the advance Presidential Communications Officer setting up the President's visit to Elmendorf Air Force Base, Anchorage, Alaska in November 1996. As the advance PCO for this trip, I showed up a day before my team was due to fly in. I flew in commercial and got a rental car to get over to the base. The White House had sent a request to the Base Commander to setup a meeting with him the day I arrived. I happened to arrive to the base about thirty minutes later then my meeting time with the Base Commander.

When I got to the gate guard post at the airbase and showed my credentials to the guard, he said "My escort was here waiting for me, and just follow them." I didn't understand what he was talking about, until he pointed to two Military Police cars next to the gate. I got a lights and siren escort to the Base Commanders building. I just had to smile, there was no need for this type of escort even with me being thirty minutes late. I was escorted into the Base Commander's conference room and there around the table was every single department head of the whole base and the Base Commander that had been waiting on me. There were 50 or more people in that conference room.

I was ushered up to the front of the table and sat down next to the Commanding General of the base and everyone turned to me and waited for me to say something. I was expecting to just meet with the Base Commander as a courtesy so I could politely tell him I was on his base and that my team would be arriving tomorrow on a military transport. This was just military etiquette when you arrive on someone else turf. I was not expecting all these folks at our first meeting.

Well, I had completed enough visits, at enough locations that I knew what I needed. Even though I wasn't prepared for a group of folks and for doing this type of briefing at this time, I went right in and explained to everyone what I needed. The Base Commander asked a lot of questions which I answered. He told me he had detailed a full squadron of support personnel to my needs, that was about 150 Airmen at my disposal for whatever I needed. I didn't have the heart to tell the Base Commander I only needed a dozen or so folks, he was trying to be so helpful.

I did give the Commander and his team a few missions that I needed done. I mentioned that my team would arrive the next morning on a C-141 Air Force transport and that if I could get some help with unloading our equipment off the plane that would be helpful. I expected a dozen folks to show up to help the next morning. But what I got was 50 or so Airmen on the tarmac first thing in the morning to help us unload. That was service.

When you asked the military to support a Presidential trip or event you always got 110% support with no questions asked, it was always "Yes Sir, what can we do for you?"

CLASSIFIED OVERSEAS MISSION

Towards my later time at The White House, when I was one of their most experienced Presidential Communications Officer, I was selected to participate in a special White House Envoy mission. The White House wanted to send an envoy to a country that the U.S. did not have diplomatic relationship with. The White House wanted to communicate face to face with this country but didn't want it in the news so this whole mission was off the books. This was a highly classified mission and was not anywhere on any official travel report or White House tasking/action list.

Because of the type of mission and where we were going, no Secret Service support was provided for this mission. They wanted to keep the mission quiet and used an all military team that they could govern under top secret orders. I was given several Marines (a Gunny Sergeant and several young troops) from the Marine support detachment, that supports The White House, as the security force for this mission. I had worked with the Marines on and off my whole military career, I have even been the commanding officer of Marines throughout my career. I thought I knew Marines, I had built a preconceived notion of jarhead Marines. This mission would totally change my opinion of young Marines, their professionals and their ability.

I hand selected my team and the equipment we would need for this mission and got ready to go. We ended up going overseas on a military transport and then cross loaded into another unmarked military transport to go to a classified location/country. We landed at a small airport in the middle of nowhere. We were met by a small group that had three car's, but no truck. We had specifically asked for a van or truck for our communications equipment and they did not bring what was agreed upon.

We had to bring with us the communications equipment that would allow top secret level communications back to the United States and the ability to send and received signed documents. We had to be self-contained because we did not know what type of environment we would be in. We brought a generator, bottled water, MREs (Meals Ready to Eat) and other equipment to meet the needs of this mission. With all the equipment we had, we needed a car or van to take this equipment with us off the airfield to the meeting location.

We landed at night for security reasons and the plane that brought us left as soon as we offloaded. There we were in the middle of nowhere, at night, with our top-secret equipment and no way to take the equipment with us. So now what, I had to make a decision on what to do. We had no choice but to leave quite a bit of the equipment. We could take some of the equipment in the cars we had, but not all of it. We would have to leave some of the top security equipment behind and that was unacceptable.

We wanted to be on the ground the shortest amount of time possible so we had to get started. We had to go with The White House envoy to the meeting location so they could get started right away. I could not leave this equipment behind. As the officer in charge of this mission I made a call to leave three of my Marines to guard our equipment. We split the equipment up, took some with us and put the other equipment aside on the tarmac where we landed. We left MREs and water for the Marine guards and we departed the area.

We did not bring communications equipment for in country use, so we would have no way of communicating with the Marines that were guarding this equipment. They were on their own for the night. We did bring weapons with us, but our orders were not to engage hostiles, to keep a very low profile, get in and get out without leaving a trace we were there. I had to give my Marines the Rules of Engagement (ROE) for their overnight stay. I told them to guard the equipment, don't let any foreign national get into or touch any of the equipment. Do not shoot back even if shot at, if it came to the point that the equipment was going to get compromised to use the thermite grenades we had and burn all the equipment in place and then escape and evade.

Other than the envoy and myself no one on the mission knew what country we were in. No one knew what the situation on the ground was other than hostile towards the United States and this was not a friendly country. I did tell everyone what direction and the distance needed to escape and evade, but that was about all my team knew.

I worked at trying to get a van or truck to the airport all night long but the country we were in would not do it. They would not drive to the airstrip area at night, they said it was not safe. I kept asking about my troops that I left behind, if it wasn't safe to drive to the airstrip was it safe for my Marines, of course it wasn't.

Finally, early in the morning the next day, the envoy mission was finished. We were able to accomplish the mission with the small amount of communications equipment we had taken with us. We returned to the small airstrip to see what had happened overnight with my troops and our equipment. When we arrived, the first thing we saw was that our equipment was not where we had left it and neither were my Marine. I thought the worst; did I just lose a couple of Marines and some top-secret equipment? Before the cars stopped rolling, the Marine Gunny Sergeant and his other Marines jumped out of the car's and started searching the area. We were all on high alert status now with guns drawn. It only took a few minutes until we found our guys and our equipment. The Marines moved all the equipment to a much better defensible location.

In the light of day, we could see much more of the airstrip where we had landed. There were some old buildings and one blown up hanger. The Marines had moved the equipment into the blown up hanger area to have a more defensible position. The Marines had been harassed all night long; they had hostile people show up out of the dark, to see who these people were on the airstrip and what stuff they had. They were asked for water and food to share. They were harassed by groups of hostiles that wanted to take their equipment, they had even been harassed by gunfire in their direction. I will not go into this more detail as it may provide too much information on the location or this mission. These Marines had been up all night long and the stress of this mission had shown on their faces when we hooked back up with them.

The Gunny Sargent took charge, deployed our other Marines and took the Marines that were there overnight to the side to get some food and water and rest. We had to wait until night time when the plane finally arrived. We got on and made it home safely with no incident. We had accomplished the mission provided secure communications for The White House Envoy.

Working with these young Marines on this mission totally changed my perception of how professional, trustworthy, and innovative young Marines can be. We had a very difficult mission in the middle of nowhere, receiving threats all night long. The actions and names of these Marines will never be known by the public, the U.S. citizens that these Marines support, but it is known by me. I cannot say enough about how these Marines met their mission, in a very hostile environment, and did not causing an international incident.

Semper-Fi! (the Marine moto – that means "Always faithful."

CHAPTER 11
VIP Tour Guide to the 18 Acres

LEARNING HOW TO BECOME A TOUR GUIDE

As I have stated in previous chapters, I had to stay on the 18 Acres (The White House ground) as the Presidential Communications Officer (PCO), duty officer for twenty-four-hour periods of time. I learned a lot about The White House just by walking around and reading the signs. I had to stay on the complex ready to do my duty, but most of times this duty was very boring. I would walk around from room to room, area to area, searching the building and the grounds to get to know my surroundings. You never know what was going to happen while you were on duty, so you had to be prepared to get from one side of the 18 Acres to the other side at a moment's notice. You had to learn all the shortcuts, all the back hallways, all the tunnels and other things in and around The White House as part of your duty. But this also led to being very educated about the grounds.

I had been shown around by some other PCO's before I started being assigned the twenty-four-hour duty. I had been shown all the official and classified things to help me do my job. I was shown the Bunker under The White House, where I would spend the night while on duty. I was shown quick ways to get around without interfering with the normal day to day operations of The White House and its staff. It was a great start at learning the grounds and learning the job as a PCO Duty Officer.

I wanted to learn more, so while I was on duty and The White House was open to tours, including private guided tours. I tagged along and heard what the tour guides had to say. It was boring to be on duty for twenty-four hours and not be able to leave, taking tours gave you something to do. The guided tours were given before and after The White House was open to the public. These guided tours were for people who paid for them and were only allowed in the same areas as the public tours with a few exceptions. The tour guides still could not take these people in many of the places of The White House I could go because they didn't have the clearance I had.

I walked around the places that the tour guides could not go and wanted to learn more about these placed. So, I purchased some books and did a lot of reading and research. After a while, I knew more about the history of The White House than most of the tour guides. Most of the POC's that had overnight duty did this type of research and education. We even made up a little cheat sheet to help us doing VIP tours when called upon.

GIVING VIP TOURS

When White House VIPs came to town, they would be shown around by someone on The White House staff. Most of the time The White House Protocol office handled these VIPs. Sometimes the Protocol office didn't have the manpower because of other events, or they knew that the PCO duty officer would be at The White House anyway on nights and weekends. They would call on the PCO duty officer to see if we could do tours for them. The mission always came first, but we did these VIP tours when the mission allowed.

As a PCO with a go anywhere badge and with my knowledge of The White House grounds I was called upon by The White House Protocol office many times. You never know who you would be giving a tour to when the Protocol office called you. I gave a tour to a Prince of some African country one time and then the next time it was the President or CEO of a multinational company. I must have given over twenty tours a year to VIPs each year I was at The White House. Everyone wanted to know the behind the scenes information, which I had. Some brought their families with them, so I made sure I had things that would keep kids entertained too. I think I could have made a living as a tour guide, because I was pretty good at it.

FAMILY AND FRIEND TOURS

I also had the ability of giving family and friends guided tours of the 18 Acres complex. I would get called by friends of friends and groups that friends had given them my name. Everyone wanted a behind the scenes tour of The White House. But I had to be very picky, on who I gave tours to. There were a lot of rules to follow and the people you had with you had to follow them 100% without fail or you would get in big trouble. I knew of a few people that were let go from their White House job not because something they did, but because of something one of their guests did. The White House was not a forgiving place, make a mistake and you were out.

When I had folks that wanted to come to The White House, I would have to get their personal information, like their social security number, and other personal data. I would have to submit this information on a special form to the Secret Service so they could do background checks on everyone I escorted on to the grounds. The background checks were pretty substantial and I told everyone this. If you didn't want me or others to know about a bad past, don't ask to come for a special VIP tour. I did have one individual that asked for a tour get turned down and the Secret Service told me why and to not associate with that individual. It was quite embarrassing for the individual that was turned down, I communicated with him and said it was up to him what he was going to tell the others in the group as to why that he could not go on the tour. Luckily almost everyone passed the background checks just fine.

The whole Gelhardt Family - VIP tour of The White House

I would meet these folks at the Uniform Secret Service guard gate on the south side of The White House, between the Old Executive Office Building (OEOB) and the West Wing of The White House. They would have to go through magnetometers and get their bags searched. They were not allowed to bring in camera's and their bags were searched for those and other things. Anyone not found to follow the rules at this point was turned away from The White House. I did have one friend, with his family, that brought a camera after I told him he could not. When he was checked, the Secret Service found the camera and escorted him off the property. I gave his wife and kids a tour as he sat outside in the car. I don't know what he told his kids about following the rules but I told him never to ask me for a favor again.

As I have already mentioned the rules were very tight. I could not give tours if the President was on the grounds, you never knew if he would be working late in the Oval Office or would be walking around The White House. I could only give tours when the President was off the 18 Acres complex. So, when the President changed his schedule at the last minute, which President Clinton did all the time, it would mess up someone coming for a tour. I had no control of this and told everyone that asked for a tour that anything could happen and they would just have to roll with it. It did happen, that I was supposed to give tours, a couple of times, and the President changed his schedule and those folks could not do the tours as scheduled. A couple of times these folks were from out of town and just had to miss the tour all together. Since I worked a twenty-four-hour tour I was usually off the next day and needed to get some rest. I felt bad about going home when I could have come back into The White House the next night and tried to do a tour if the President was off the compound. But I warned everyone that a VIP Tour was a favor to most of them and anything could happen.

Outside of Oval Office – taken from the South Lawn

I warned everyone that there were cameras everywhere and that the Secret Service was always watching. I also had to brief all the folks that came on the tours that they would have to do exactly what I said, when I said it and that they were not to ask questions, just do what I said. I told them you never know when an alarm would go off or when a dignitary may walk by. They would have to move out of the way, press against the wall and allow those folks that were doing their job to move by them. This often happened during these tours. You never knew what was going on in The White House and what dignitary may be visiting a staff person, etc. You couldn't do the tours when the President was in The White House but that didn't mean others were not around. You would see Senators or Congressmen, and a couple of times the VP walked by, but the tour group was not supposed to talk to these folks and just move out of their way. It did provide for good memories for those that got a little extra during their VIP tour by seeing an important person.

It was great when it all worked out. People really loved taking the tour and seeing all the behind the scenes items. Let me point out, a few items that I think are unique at The White House. Today you can go on the web and find a lot of White House facts and knowledge, but back in the mid-1990's the internet was not yet to the point it is today.

VIP TOUR HIGHLIGHTS

THE EAGLE – The Seal of the President of the

United States is a symbol with an eagle in the middle of it. The eagle holds thirteen arrows in its left talon (foot) that represents the need to sometimes go to war to protect the nation. The right talon (foot) holds thirteen olives and thirteen leaves to represent peace. In the old days, the head of the eagle on the presidential symbol would change from looking to the right and to the left. If the United States was at war the head of the eagle would be turned towards the arrows. If the United States was at peace the head of the eagle would be turned towards the olive branches. This changed in 1945 when President Truman began making important changes throughout the U.S. government, including changes to the Presidential Seal. He ordered that the eagle be changed to face the olive branch, rather than the arrows. He wanted the seal to reflect an emphasis on the pursuit of peace.

There are three areas in The White House where the Presidential Seal has the eagle with its head turning towards the arrows and not the olive branches. The other ninety-seven Presidential Seals at The White House have the eagles head facing the olive branches.

This would be one of the items I would ask the kids on the tour to look for, "Can you find the eagle with the head turned towards the arrows?" One of the spot's that has the eagle with its head turned towards the arrows is the cornerstone of the East Wing, which was built during the second World War. This cornerstone is on the northeast corner of the building, you cannot see this on the regular public tours. You have to take a private tour with the right access to get to that spot on the grounds.

East Wing Corner Stone 1942 with Eagle facing the arrows my kids Kris and David with me

The second eagle is above the Diplomatic Reception Room. In 1903, this bronze seal was embedded in the floor in The White House entrance hall. President Truman dislike seeing visitors walking on the seal and had it moved during the renovation of 1948-1952 and now is in a frame in the main entrance area to The White House.

The third eagle is on the Resolute desk that is in the Oval office

RESOLUTE DESK – This is a large, nineteenth-century partners desk used by many Presidents in the Oval office. This desk was a gift from Queen Victoria to President Rutherford Hays in 1880. There is famous picture of JFK and his son, John peeking out from the bottom center portion of the desk, there is a movable center portion. There were also some famous discussions about where Nixon kept his recording devices (the Nixon tapes) within the desk. This desk was made from the timbers of the HMS (Her Majesties Ship) Resolute, an abandoned British ship discovered by an American vessel and returned to the Queen of England as a token of friendship and goodwill. The Queen took timbers from the ship and made a desk for the President and sent it as a sign of good will back to the U.S.

The original desk was a double pedestal desk with an open center, but it was modified during President Roosevelt's term with a hinged removable front panel in order to hide President Roosevelt's leg braces or wheel chair. The panel that was added features the Presidential Seal. The seal on the desk is one of only three seals out of ninety-seven Presidential Seals at The White House that have the eagles head turned towards the thirteen arrows in the eagles left talon, because this eagle was added during a time of war (WWII).

The desk was again modified by being raised a few inches for President Reagan. He was hitting his knees on the desk, so in 1986 they put on a new base that raised the desk to give him more space.

THE PRESIDENTIAL MANSION – Do
you know why they call the house that the Presidents lives in "The White House?" When the Presidential mansion was first built and was the biggest building in the United States. It was gray on the outside and the stones used to build the mansion were sandstone that were gray in color. There was a lot of discussion on what to the call the house that the President lived in and that has changed over the years until President Theodore Roosevelt used the words The White House on his stationary in 1901. Why was the mansion changed from its gray stone color to white? Very simply when The White House was burned down by the British, they could not clean the stones enough to get it back to one original gray color. So, they painted over the burned stones with whitewash. There you go a White House, to cover the burn spots.

The White House was built in 1792, burned down in 1814, rebuilt in 1817, the renovated in 1902, and the last renovation was in 1952.

BURN SPOTS – Did you realize that the British
invaded Washington D.C., the capital of the United States, during the War of 1812? On August 24, 1814, the British forces set fire to many public buildings including The White House. About the only thing in The White House that is original from the first White House is the panting of George Washington and some silver candlesticks. First Lady Dolly Madison, when she saw the British coming,

was able to save these things. But those are the only original items in The White House today.

The White House, even though it has been restored and renovated several times has the original outside stones. There are several places out of the view of the general public that the original gray stones can be seen, with the fire burn marks still on them. The two places that I know of where you can see the burn spots are, one up in the Presidents residency, that I heard was up there to remind the President of the history of this great house. Then there is one down on the ground floor under the front entrance to the north side of The White House out of view from the general public. But the people that work at The White House can see this mark and remember the history of this old house. I would take visitors to this spot and talk about the naming of The White House, the burning down of The White House, and show them the history still marked on the walls of this great old mansion.

UNDER THE FRONT LAWN – Also,

when I was at the burn spot under the north entrance to The White House. I would show them the flower shop, and the wood working shop. The ground floor and the basement areas (two basement levels) held all the back workings of The White House. The White House was a self-contained little city. If something broke they had a full woodshop and a full maintenance area for people on staff that could fix or make almost anything you wanted. These were very small areas, think of a one car garage for the wood working shop and another one car garage for the maintenance shop. There was also a flower shop, again about the size of a one car garage under the front lawn area. They would cut all the flowers and put all the arrangements out, fresh flowers almost every day and for every occasion. There was storage under the front lawn and in the basements, chairs, tables, decorations, stages, lighting, etc. This stuff would be taken out used and then carefully stacked back into a nook or cranny under The White House, under the front lawn fountain.

There is a large area under the front fountain on the North Lawn that includes a two-lane bowling alley, that is between the flower shop and the wood working shop. The President would come down under the fountain in the basement and bowl sometimes. There is also a worker's walkway under the North entrance (the main entrance) to The White House. This walkway is out of sight from the street and is used to deliver food to the kitchen and to deliver supplies to The White House. This is a favorite place for me to take VIP visitors. It shows the back workings of The White House. We can pop into the one of the three floors of kitchens. The kitchen is broken up with different work spaces on three different floors, all of which are really small for a mansion this size. My house at home has a kitchen about the same size as one floor of the kitchen. Most times, I would not take folks into the kitchen because something was always being cooked or going on and there was just no space to show folks around in this area.

There are a lot of people that support The White House that were not military. They are just regular people doing their jobs day in and day out to make sure this great house and its occupants show the rest of the world what America is all about. I got to get to know a lot of these people as I walked around on duty. I would love to talk to them about their jobs and how they liked working at The White House.

Almost every single one of them said they loved supporting their country. Presidents come and go; political parties come and go – but to support the ideals of the Presidency to be the support staff that makes The White House function was an amazing job to have. Many of these people you have never heard about have worked in the Presidents house for years, administration after administration. What dedication.

THE PRESS POOL – I talked about the Press
Pool and my duties managing the Audio Visional, in Chapter 5. I talked about some of the lay out and size then. I always found it funny how the TV shows and the movies show the press area at The White House. This area is extremely small. Back when President Roosevelt was in office, he had a pool put in the area between The White House and the West Wing. This area, with this indoor pool, was used by Roosevelt and Presidents after him until a heated pool was built outside just south of the Oval Office on the South Lawn area, next to the tennis and basketball courts. No one can see all these areas because of the trees and foliage planted around this area.

So why do they call it, "The White House Press Pool?" I would ask every tour that I did, can you guess? Well the Press is actually sitting in the area where the indoor swimming pool was in The White House. The actual Press Pool area is in the old covered indoor pool area between The White House and the West Wing. When President Johnson decided to bring the press back onto The White House grounds to try and get better press for the Vietnam War, he put the press in the tiny area that used to be the indoor pool.

The Press Pool area, were the press sit and ask questions

A fun fact, however, is when this happened and the press got this area. Because the press pool area was the only way to get to the West Wing staying inside. Now, for the President to get from the residence in The White House to the Oval Office every day, rain or shine, hot or cold, he has to walk outside through the Rose Garden area. There is a covered walkway, but he has to go outside every day to get to the Oval Office.

I was able, during the afterhours tours to take people into the Press Pool area and let them get pictures behind the lectern with The White House symbol on the curtain behind them. I would ask one of the night press people to take the pictures for me. They were happy to do this, because most of the time nothing was going on at The White House because the President was off the 18 Acres at this time. This worked out well and people were able to have a souvenir of their tour.

Press Room tour with my brothers – here is all three of us

The space under the speaking area of the Press Pool is even smaller then you may think. It is the actual pool bottom and is used by the major news networks. They use small cubicles about the size of 5x5. You could not even lie down in them they were so small. There was cable everywhere as the original press pool was not set up for the multi-media of today's world. The area downstairs was so small and tight that I didn't take anyone down stairs. I just saw a nice PBS documentary on the Press Pool area, I am sure you can google it and get more information. Also under a recent renovation of The White House they expanded the basement and the area under the Press Pool to give the press more space.

Not only were the press allowed to use the Press Pool area they also had areas with cameras and small canopies set up outside on the North Lawn to the right of the front of The White House. The press had cameras set up outside 24/7.

They were always ready to do a camera shot of their reporter with the front of The White House over their shoulder in the background. When you watch TV today you see this shot all the time.

THE BUNKER – As I stated in Chapter 3, there is
a bunker under the East Wing area. The bunker area under the East Wing has a standard office double door in the front area. You would never know this was the way down to the bunker if you didn't already know. You have to have the right code to enter those office doors and off course the U.S. Secret Service had a camera on that door and when it was open an alarm would go off indicating to the Secret Service that someone was walking through that door. Plus, the Uniformed Secret Service locker room and break area was in this very same location. So, there was usually always someone on break in that room that could respond in a second if someone tried to get through these doors that was not supposed to.

It was a thrill for people to come up to these doors and for me to open them and let them look down the hallway. I was not allowed to take anyone into this area unless I cleared it way ahead of time. I did take my family down the hallway when I had a tour with them. I showed them the bunker door and some other areas in the basement. It is a typical nuclear type bunker door with radiation showers at the entrance and everything else you would think a bunker front door would have. Of course, you either have to have the code or be buzzed in to get into this space.

Most visitors found this information and my discussion about this area as a highlight to their tour as everyone always wants to know classified stuff or things that others don't know. It's our nature to ask questions and find out information that others don't have. I never revealed any classified information. But I did tell people that this was where I slept when I stayed the night at The White House. I spent a lot of time in the bunker. I learned everything I could about this space.

THE OLD EXECUTIVE OFFICE BUILDING

Part of the 18 Acres complex that makes up the secure White House compound is the Old Executive Office Building (OEOB). The Old Executive Office Building was commissioned by President Grant and was built during the period of 1871-1888. The building was originally called the State, War, and Navy Building because it hosed those departments. The Army and Navy moved out of this building when the Pentagon was built during WWII. There are some great pictures hanging in the hallway showing the use of the building over time. There are pictures of people in desks in the hallway as the building was bulging at the seams during World War I and II. That was why they built the Pentagon, that we know today that holds the Department of Defense (which is what the War Department turned into).

This building was built in the French Second Empire style and is one of the last remaining building in the U.S. of that style. You just know that history was made in this building and now it was your turn to be part of the current history. It has wide hallways, high ceilings, and doors with transom windows above them. This building was built before air conditioners were made and that shows in its architecture. However, the building is built so well that the air moves through the building very well, even though they have retrofitted the building with air condition, it doesn't really need it. You just need to look down at the tiles on the floor to see all the wear and tear over the years to feel the history that was made here.

In 1981, plans began to restore all the "Secretary of …" suites. The main office of the Secretary of the Navy was restored in 1987 and is now used as the Ceremonial Office of the Vice President. It has a lot of Navy pictures and boats in showcases. The VP Ceremonial Office was used several times for things like military promotions and awards ceremonies. This is where all the military that worked on the 18 Acres had their ceremonies. On the days of a military ceremonies many of the military that worked on The White House grounds would wear their uniforms to the 18 Acres. It was one of the only days you got to see how many military folks actually work on The White House grounds.

CHAPTER 12
The Perks

Working at The White House was a rough job with a lot of stress and very long hours, but there were a few unique perks, this chapter talks about those perks.

PRESIDENTIAL SERVICE BADGE

You can easily see if someone was the best in their service just by looking at their uniform. If you saw someone wearing the Presidential Service Badge (PSB) or the Vice-President Service Badge (VPSB), you knew they were the best! Look at the picture in my Bio and you can see the PSB on my right breast pocket under my name tag. This is one of the most prestigious badge you can earn in the military.

Presidential Service Badge

After working at The White House for a year in support of the President or Vice-President, military members are awarded the Presidential Service Badge (PSB) or the Vice-President Service Badge (VPSB). The PSB is a badge that has the eagle from the Presidential Seal on it on a blue background trimmed in gold. The VPSB has the eagle from the Presidential Seal on it but has a white background trimmed in gold. The VPSB is usually only given to senior non-commissioned officers (NCOs) that have provided the VP with direct support and not worked on the Presidential side of support. These two badges are a very big deal when worn on your uniform, everyone knows that you worked at The White House just by looking at your uniform. It implies you are part of the very best the services have to offer, since the selection process is so hard, this makes these two badges very coveted badges. The badges are so rare to receive that they are all numbered on the back and highly accounted for. You cannot just go out and purchase one, you have to be awarded one by The White House. You are almost guaranteed a promotion to the next higher rank or two after successfully completing a tour of duty at The White House. Even with the extensive selection process about 25% of people that get selected to work at The White House don't last a full year and do not receive their PSB. The White House duty positions are very demanding, very hard, with long hours, and extreme pressure/stress that I do not even have the words to explain. There are so many ways for you to mess up that I am not surprised that more people get fired before the end of the year. The normal length of duty at The White House is two years, because of the operational tempo and because of the extreme stress. By rotating people out every two years it gives these highly sought-after positions more openings. This provides more people the opportunity to serve in these coveted positions. With high stress comes high reward and so it is with working at The White House.

KENEDY CENTER TICKETS

When you work inside The White House, you get the opportunity to ask for Presidential tickets to events. The White House receives tickets for many different types of events. If they are not used by the President and or senior staff, they can be used by other White House employees. The best example of this and the one I liked and used the most was tickets for the Presidential Box at the Kennedy Center. Each one of the theaters in the Kennedy Center has a Presidential Box. These were sought after tickets especially for high rated shows playing at the Kennedy Center. I learned the system; learned who to go to, learned that I could actually apply for tickets and sometimes get them. You had to fill out a form way in advance, stating the reason you wanted the tickets how many tickets needed, etc. They often gave the tickets, to a person that had an anniversary or birthday or special event in their life.

To get the tickets for the Presidential box, you had to sign and read a form that talks about behavior, be on the very best behavior; drinking (do not get drunk), timing (never be late), be in your seats before the show starts. There was a whole protocol sheet to read of the does and don'ts. If you were a military member, you were asked to wear your dress uniform, if you were a civilian you were asked to wear a tuxedo. There were eight seats in the Presidential Box. You never knew who else you would be sitting with. There was some excitement to that too. An ambassador, a head of a major corporation, you just never knew who would sit next to you.

The envelope that you get the tickets in

I was lucky enough to get tickets several times to the Kennedy Center. I remember for my fifteen-year wedding anniversary, I was able to get tickets. This was the first time after I had started working at The White House that my wife really got a benefit out of my long hours. We got all dressed up, me in my Army Mess Dress Uniform with all my medals and my badges, my wife was in a long gown, we looked great together. I was able, through a friend, to get reservations at the Capital Club for dinner. That was an expensive dinner, but fun, and then went to the Kennedy Center for the evening play. It was a magical evening that not many others could say they could do.

It was our first time in the Kennedy Center building and we did not know where to go when we got there and I had to ask someone for directions. It is kind of funny when that happened. I showed the employee at the front desk our tickets and she said to hold on for a second that she would have to check something. It was my first time using the tickets and I thought, are we late, did I do something wrong, what didn't I do right? But just then the head usher came around to meet with us and said to follow him. He personally escorted us to a private back door and through to the private entrance to the Presidential Box. We felt like royalty! When you grow up poor like I did you are not used to people going out of their way, tripping over themselves, to provide you with five-star service. This usher didn't know who we were as people, but he knew that only special people sat in the Presidential Box and he treated us like a king and queen.

The Presidential Box was very posh, it had a sitting area back behind the seats, its very own bathroom, had a full bar that was stocked and there was food laid out. The food was very good and fancy food, but we were already full from dinner. But I had to have some food to taste what rich people eat. I opened the bar refrigerator and there was a little of everything in there. I noticed some mini-Champaign bottles that had the Presidential Seal on them. I took a few for souvenirs and still have them today. Several other people showed up in the box that evening, all White House staff support personnel with their spouses, no celebrities. We sat down in the box seats a few minutes before the show started. Everyone was looking at us in the box, it was like who are those people? All the other boxes wanted to see who was in the Presidential Box behind the President's Seal, that was on the balcony in front of the box, designating the Presidential Box. That was a unique feeling for me, as a service member, we are taught to serve, do your job, stay in the background. It was a new feeling to be the center of so many people's attention.

Champaign bottle from the Presidential Suite

My wife and I went to the Kennedy Center and sat in the Presidential Box several times during my time at The White House. The absolute awe that I had that first time never really went away. I was always thankful for getting tickets and always did my part in the box to show the right respect for the President and for taking his place and holding up the honor of sitting in his spot. My wife and I did meet some interesting people in the box over the years. Some celebrates, some other staff members, and every now and then some extraordinary people that the President had brought into town for a ceremony, or event. You know the folks you see on TV behind the President when he signs a bill or is talking about a topic, these were always down to earth people that I very much enjoyed helping when it was their first time in the Presidential Box learning their way around and what to do.

EASTER EGG ROLL

Not only did my wife see some benefits from me working at The White House such as going to the Kennedy Center, my kids also were able to receive some benefits. The benefit they liked the most was the Easter event on the South Lawn. Every year the President and First Lady hold a large Easter party on the South Lawn of The White House. You have to receive an invitation to be part of this event. Having staff members children as the primary crowd for this event, make sure that the kids would behave and that there was always someone to go to, to help with children corrections. At least that is the way it looked to me. It also makes it much easier for the Secret Service, since all the parents that accompany the kids onto the South Lawn are already cleared to be on The White House grounds. I got my kids tickets to go every year.

This was one of the times the kids didn't mind coming to The White House. My wife got to dress the kids up, especially our girl Kristine, in her Easter finest with an Easter hat. The kids could play and even get dirty, if that happened. The whole family liked this event. The kids looked forward to this event for the first couple of years. They were just the right age and enjoyed themselves.

The Easter Egg Roll was the best part. If they won the Easter Egg Roll they would receive a wooded souvenir Easter Egg. I still have a couple of these Easter eggs today.

The kids loved to win the race and get the eggs. Over the years the Easter event weekend got too big and there were to many kids that came. Over time, we stopped going to this event, along with many other events. The newness had rubbed off and the crowds would be too big.

David, Kris and I at the Easter Egg Hunt in 1996

Souvenir Easter Eggs from 1996

4th OF JULY

One year, I got tickets to watch the 4th of July on the South Lawn of The White House. I still have these tickets as a treasure to remember this fun day. I didn't like going downtown during big events, the crowds were just too large. However, we thought we should do this one event - 4th of July on The White House lawn. The South Lawn of

The White House is bigger than it looks, you can fit a lot of people on there and still have space. I did my normal request for tickets, I had learned the system, who to be nice to, who to ask, when to ask, and I received tickets for the whole family.

4th of July invitation to site on the South Lawn

I decided to take the subway downtown. We parked south of town at the end of the subway line and took our blanket and picnic basket on the subway. It was a great idea at 1:00 PM early on the 4th of July. The subway was crowded but not too bad. We took the subway down to the Mall area and walked over to The White House. People were already staking out their spots on the Mall, there were blankets everywhere. That was ok, we would be on The White House lawn and would not have to deal with the masses or so I thought.

We got to The White House, showed our tickets, went through security, and there we were. Wide open spaces on the South Lawn where we setup our blanket in some shade and had a late day picnic. At The White House, there was music playing out of speakers on the South Lawn and other families and kids were showing up. My kids had a great time running around and playing with the other kids. This was one of the times my kids enjoyed coming to The White House and not worrying about having to behave (until later).

Later that evening, when more people showed up and started putting down blankets on the South Lawn I looked over to the next blanket over and saw Linda Carter the actress of "Wonder Women" fame. We shared some niceties, some hello's but I never really got to talk to her. I think my wife had a lot to do with distracting me from talking to Wonder Women? The President and First Lady came out to the South Lawn and gave a short speech before the fireworks. Thanking the people that were there, said some other things and visited with some high-ranking VIPs, of course they didn't take the time to talk to the little people, like me.

The fireworks were what you would expect from a National Capital, they were outstanding. The best part of it was the Marine Band had setup on the South Lawn and where playing music before the fireworks, and also during the fireworks. It was great to have the band playing and the fireworks going off, the kids running around and not having to worry about security and the crowds.

When the fireworks were over, we should have stayed on the South Lawn for an extra hour or more and let the crowds go down, but we were all tired and wanted to go home. We gathered up our stuff and since we had not driven downtown, we headed for the closest subway station for our ride out of town. But, so did every other person on the Washington Mall area. I have never been scared riding the subway, until this evening. The crowds were pushing everyone forward right next to the tracks and the trains. This was worse than a concert or a stampede of animals. My wife and kids were actually scared for their lives as we waited for the next train. I was too! I was afraid the mob behind us would push us on the tracks before the train got there. The crowd control from the city police was nowhere to be seen. This was a very harrowing experience that my kids to this day still remember and talk about.

WHITE HOUSE GIFT STUFF

When you have access to the 18 Acres (The White House Grounds) in the basement of the Old Executive Office Building (OEOB) there was a Secret Service gift store. This store tucked away in the basement at one of the back corners. It is this tiny little place that had all this Secret Service and White House knickknacks. This was a great place to end a tour (if it was open) and let people purchase something inside The White House grounds. I purchased a lot of gifts for family and friends down there.

The White House Communications Agency also had a store for members inside its main headquarters building in

Anacostia Navel Air Station. But, this building was a classified building and you had to have a reason to enter it and be escorted. So, the Secret Service Store on the 18 Acres was the place most people went to get White House stuff that you could not get anywhere else.

There was also a White House Historical Association stand that was open on the basement level of The White House between the East Wing and the main house. This would be rolled out during the public tours and it also has some White House knickknacks to include the annual White House Christmas Ornament. This was a must for my family, we purchased a White House Christmas ornament every year since I worked there. You can now purchase them online. In the old days you could only get them at The White House but things have changed over time.

Lastly, several of the offices during the holiday season would sell items to make money for their party funds. The White House Airlift Operations would sell Christmas ornaments with AF1 and HMX1 on them, you could also pick up some very nice White House style prints. This was a typical going away gift for most folks that worked within the Military at The White House. I am proud to have a print of HMX-1 taking off from the South Lawn, signed by the artist thanking me for my service at The White House.

CHRISTMAS AT THE WHITE HOUSE

The very best event held at The White House that is open to the family members, is the Christmas Open House. There is one evening set aside that The White House is closed to all except the military support to The White House and their families.

This is the one time you could bring your family into The White House and take pictures and show them around. It was all decorated for the holidays and the house looked fantastic. Normally, you were not allowed to bring cameras to work or duty and take pictures. If your family visited you at The White House for some reason, you could not take them to the main White House building. You would meet them at security and go over to the Old Executive Office building. This one time of year your family could come to the East Wing, West Wing and to the main White House and walk around taking pictures, see where you worked and who you worked for.

The White House ready for Christmas

President Kennedy portrait and a Christmas Tree

As I said in Chapter 3, Military Support to The White House, there are a lot of military members that not only support The White House on the grounds of the 18 Acres but that also support outside of the 18 Acres. Air Force One members almost never got to go on the grounds of The White House, they just were not cleared to do that. But, on this one day, they could and bring their families. The military members of The White House Garage, and HMX-1 and others that supported The White House year-round but didn't have the same access as I did. With my Go

Anywhere badge, I had in fact seen more of The White House then most of these people and I ended up being a tour guide during this open house. I didn't mind, most of these military members showed me around their areas, such as the tour I received of Air Force One, and other facilities.

My family and I got all dressed up, the kids didn't like that, and went down to The White House again for another function. We walked the grounds and I showed them around and we took pictures of us all with The White House Christmas Tree behind us. It was a very nice evening.

The President came down from the resident portion of The White House on the top floors and said a few words thanking his military support staff. You could tell he didn't want to be there, President Clinton and the First Lady treated the military staff like servants, that were way below their position. We were just servants to do the Presidents and First Ladies bidding. He had no concern for the hours we put in, for the scarifies we made. He just didn't seem to care. I had been told by folks that had worked at The White House, for other administrations that other Presidents would come down meet the families, take pictures with the families and be genuinely thankful for all the military had done for the President. But not President Clinton. I know the man was busy and had a lot on his plate, but this was a big slap in the face to all the military members that worked so hard for the President. I guess I should just be happy that he took ten minutes to come down and talk to us at all?

CHRISTMAS CONCERTS IN D.C.

This was not a White House perk, but a perk for living in D.C. during the holidays where there were a lot of things you could do. Almost every year when we lived in D.C. we would fill up our December weekends by going to the free military concerts, given by the Army, Navy, and Air Force. These were fantastic shows that you didn't have to pay a dime for, they were all free and open to the public, outstanding signers, and musicians that these services had. I knew these were coming every year and got my tickets as soon as the ticket information was open, so we almost always had up front seats. My family really enjoyed these shows. Several years in a row, the concerts were held at the Daughters of the American Revolution Hall that was only a block from The White House. This was a great venue, with patriotic pictures on the walls and was decorated great for the holidays.

WHITE HOUSE CHRISTMAS CARDS

During the Christmas season, the President and First Lady sent out Christmas Cards. All the support staff at The White House get a card from the first family thanking us for our work that year and rejoicing over the holiday season. Not only did we get a small Christmas Card, but we would be sent a large print of the Christmas card.

Being on the list to receive a large print was a matter of pride and stature, that mean you were a real supporter to the President (and/or the office).

These prints are so coveted that during my divorce from my first wife (after I left my White House duties) she demanded one in the divorce settlement. I was glad to give her one as a reminder for her, of her support to me during my time working at The White House. I contacted a friend of mine that was still at The White House and told them of the situation and was able to get a replace the one I give to my ex-wife.

Here is one of my four large Christmas Card Prints

I still have four prints and Christmas Cards, from the four years I was there at The White House, hanging in my office today. I look at these and remember my years working at The White House, they bring back great and happy memories of the four and half years I spent working within the walls of that great building.

PRESIDENTIAL LETTERS/NOTES

Another thing that you can get from The White House is signed Presidential Letters or Notes for special events. Anyone from outside The White House can write into The White House and request a Presidential letter or note card. The Presidents staff gets so many of these that just because you request it doesn't mean you will get it. But if you work at The White House and hand deliver your request to the right person you will get one.

THE WHITE HOUSE

WASHINGTON

June 19, 1997

LTC Mark D. Gelhardt, Sr., USA
3850 Appaloosa Drive
Woodbridge, Virginia 22192

Dear Mark:

    Happy 40th Birthday! Hillary joins me in extending warmest congratulations on this special day. We hope you have a memorable celebration and every happiness in the year ahead.

Sincerely,

Bill Clinton

Letter from the President for my 40th birthday

I have several Happy Birthday notes signed by the President on White House stationary. Of course, the President himself doesn't sign these, they are all done by machine, but it is still kind of neat to get these. I have received several for my daughter and son's birthdays, for my Anniversary's and for my own birthday. I looked at the one I received for turning 40 years old and think back now. I was just 40 years old and working at The White House.

That was the peak of my career, I was doing something important for my country, I was making a difference! It's like wining the Olympic Medal at the age of sixteen, then what do you do for the rest of your life, is it all downhill? No, it's not! I may have been doing great things that made a difference at 40, but I have had a great life since doing other things, meeting other goals. But I still like looking back at these signed letters and notes from the President. If nothing else it shows that I really was at The White House doing things back then, I have the proof.

STATE VISIT TICKETS

I was also able to get tickets for official State Visit Ceremonies on the South Lawn of The White House. Several of the State Visits I was working and could not participate in viewing the ceremonies, but there were a couple that I was off duty those days and got tickets to go. Most of these visits were during the work/school week and I would ask my wife to come with me. A couple of times I got enough tickets to have the kids come along too. I was ready to pull them out of school to go see one of these events. I think I got tickets for three or four state visits. But for one reason or another my wife didn't want to go and the kids had something going on at school. After four and half years at The White House my family never saw this fantastic pageantry.

When this happened, I would always switch with someone that was on duty and give them the tickets so they could bring their family to the event. It got to the point where my wife and kids had, had enough of my working at The White House. I put in a lot of hours and every time they came to The White House, they did not see the President being supportive of the military.

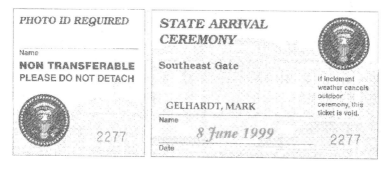

Ticket for a State Arrival Ceremony on the South Lawn

DO WE HAVE TO GO TO THE WHITE HOUSE AGAIN?

Over the four and half years I worked at The White House the kids got more opportunities to come to The White House then they wanted. They knew when they came that daddy's job was on the line and that they would have to behave for the full time they were at The White House. They did not like the restrictions that were put on them when they visited. They would have to get dressed up, they would have to be on their best behavior, etc. My family did not feel the support for the military and for their father/husband.

Can you imagine your kids/family not wanting to be a part of history? Here I was working at The White House and my wife had lost the desire to support me and my kids had lost the thrill of going to The White House. This was the time I started to consider that I had been working at The White House too long. It had taken a toll on my marriage, I had not been able to support my kids in after school events the way I would have liked to. It was time to try and save my marriage and time to get back to my kids. It was time to leave my White House job and get back to my family.

My kids, later in life would tell me that they wished they paid better attention to what I did and the events I brought them too. They wished they could remember more of their dad's days at The White House. Part of the reason I am writing this book is to provide my kids a written history of some of the stories of their dad and some of the events I took part in.

CHAPTER 13
Leaving The White House

Military officers at The White House have a two-year commitment and then you get moved to a new job, in a new unit. That is just part of the military life, moving. I had been at The White House for two two-year tours and they had asked me to stay for a third two-year tour. I just could not do it; the stress was tremendous, I turned down the third tour. I got ready to end my tour at The White House. When you know you are about to leave, sometimes you can get a few extra perks.

ASKED TO STAY

I got to the end of my second two-year tour (four years) at The White House and it was time for me to go, I was ready to leave. However, the Commander started to talk to me about what was next for me and my family? He approached me and asked me to stay for another tour to take over all operations for The White House Communications Agency, to basically be the Chief Operating Officer for WHCA. This was a great honor, to be asked to do this. I was flabbergasted that they would even offer this to me. Remember, I am an HR guy and an IT guy I am not a communications specialist and they wanted me to run all communications operations both within The White House and with the President on the road. I was humbled and really gave this offer a lot of thought, I would never get this type of offer again.

In the end, my family had put up with me working at The White House for over four years already. I worked ungodly hours, I traveled a lot, I didn't miss many birthday or holidays, but I was missing what life was all about. Life is not all about work, it is about a work life balance, I did not have this. I enjoyed my time at The White House more than I can say in words in this book. I would go back and do it again right now, given the opportunity. But my wife and I were having some troubles and I wanted to do whatever I could to save my marriage, so I turned down the job. It was time to move on to another job that would be less stressful and less time consuming.

HOMETOWN TRIP

When you start working at The White House, you just take the trips that are assigned to you and don't ask questions. After you have been there a while and understand the system and the right people to talk to, you can influence what trips you get assigned to. You can get your name pulled off of one trip and put on another trip, you can jump the roster and influence the system. This does not work all the time, but when you are a short timer (about ready to leave the job), you have much more influence. People know you are about to leave and want to help you out if they can.

One of the unwritten rules, is if the President is going to your hometown or where your family lives, the Operations folks try and put you on those trips. When you are a short timer and the President is going to your hometown people bend over backwards to put you on those trips. The whole time I was at The White House, the President had never had a trip down to South Florida where my parents lived and where I grew up. But, when I was a short timer and was going to leave The White House, the President was going to take a trip to West Palm Beach, Florida, in South Florida near where my parents lived.

I mentioned this to the Operations folks that put the folks on the trip and they bumped someone else off the trip and put me on it. I was more experienced and had the highest certifications for travel than any Presidential Communications Officer had and they usually saved the senior folks, like me, for the hardest trips; like going to Moscow and going to Beijing, both of which I was the lead on. But like I said, they made an exception for me. They actually asked me which position I would like to fill, from being in charge of the whole trip or just one of the subordinate positions. I picked a subordinate position that would give me the most fixability in my schedule.

I told my mother that I was on the trip with the President coming down to West Palm Beach and asked her what she would like to do? You see I was senior enough in the pecking order that I could make things happen. Did she want to go to the Presidential event, or meet the President, or get a tour of Air Force One, etc. She was so excited that her baby boy was going to be back home with the President and that I had made it in life. I had become a man that she could be proud of. I hope she was bursting at the seams with pride about her son.

I got my hometown trip, I worked the system, I was going to be in charge of the hotel/base of operations site. I would setup hotel with equipment to support this day trip to West Palm Beach by the President. We would setup communications and information technology equipment at a hotel close to the venue and support the US Secret

Service and The White House staff out of the base of operations site (Hotel).

SEA SCOUT SHIP 307 PRESIDENTIAL TOUR

When I found out that I was going to be down close to my hometown with the President, I contacted my old Scout Master, Mr. John Leaser. I could not believe after all these years this great man was still giving back of himself and was still running an Explorer Scout program, Sea Scout Ship 307, out of Boca Raton, Florida. He had moved up the scout chain of command and was doing a lot for the scout district now, but he still had his hands in my old Sea Scout Ship 307. I do not think I would have made it to The White House or even made it in life if it was not for Mr. John Leaser. This man was a father figure to me, this man changed my life. The Sea Scout unit help me get through my teenage years without going down the wrong path in life. I had to pay back this man and help other kids that were now in the Sea Scout unit. I told him I was going to be in West Palm Beach with the President and I would like to give a tour of several things to the Scouts.

I have to take a little side trip here. I have to tell you about this man. Scout Master John Leaser was a Vietnam Veteran, a Marine with tattoos, a short man and yes round man, but a very large man in life. One day when I was a young teen (fourteen, I think) I was riding my motorcycle out in the woods with a couple of other kids. We ran across this troop of kids camping and thought it would be a good idea to ride through the camp and knock down all the tents and mess the place up. What a stupid kid thing to do, but that was me at that age. We rode through the camp really messed it up and kept dirt bike riding for another hour or so. When we decided we were done and were heading back home, we went to see if the campsite was all setup again. We would ride through and knock everything down again. We got the campsite and it was all set back up, so we started riding through the camp to knock everything down again. Just then a man stepped out of one of the tents. He was short five foot something, he was big and round, had round muscle arms with a short sleeve shirt on and you could see the tattoos. He had an axe handle in his hands (no axe head) just the piece of wood and he stood there in front of us not moving just tapping the axe handle in his hand. We stopped dead in our tracks. He walked over to us and didn't yell at us, didn't turn us into the cops, he just talked to us. He asked if we had seen anyone else riding bikes around because someone earlier had ridden through the camp and knocked it down. I do not to this day know how he did it, but he talked a couple of us into camping out that night with the scouts. This man changed my life, he was different than most adults I knew, he cared about kids, about helping, about honor, country, and about making a difference. I would not be the man I am today, on the path I took if it was not for Mr. Leason's!

When I met Mr. Leaser and gave the Scouts a tour of the Presidential event, all the behind the scenes stuff, he asked me to call him John, I just could not do that. I had to much respect for this man, he will always be Mister Leaser to me. A year or so later after I gave a tour to the scout troop in West Palm Beach. I was asked to speak at Mr. John Leasers funeral, which I gratefully did. I am not known to have much emotion, after all the years in the military and all the things I have seen, I thought I had hidden my emotions away, until that day. Trying to speak at Mr.

Leaser's funeral was one of the hardest things I had ever done and my emotions did not allow me to finish my speech.

God Bless you Mr. Leaser, may you rest in peace!

It was great fun to give the Scout unit a tour of the Presidential event venue, behind the stage, let them stand at the Presidential Lectern and take pictures with the Presidential Seal on the lectern. I showed them the Presidential Limo, code named the Beast. I let them sit in the limo and take pictures standing by it. I showed them the hotel setup that we had for The White House. I got them a briefing by the US Secret Service about security for the President. I also got them front line standing room for the Air Force One arrival at the Airport so they could all see the President get off of Air Force One and get into the motorcade. I hope I changed one of these young kids lives, as Mr. Leaser had changed mine.

PHOTO WITH THE PRESIDENT

I do have several photos with the President as proof that I worked at The White House. It is actually unique for a military member working at The White House to have multiple photos with the President. We had a strict no photo policy, you were not allowed to take pictures while on duty. This means I did a lot of stuff and don't have pictures or proof that I was actually there. You have to remember this was in the 1990's and cellphones were just coming out and the cellphones that were out did not have cameras on them. This wasn't even the age of digital cameras and photo's. This was the time of 35mm cameras and film and sending your pictures off to be developed. Operational security was the primary reason we were not supposed to have cameras with us and take pictures on duty. Who would screen the pictures to make sure no classified material was on the photo?

There was an official White House photographer that went around with the President everywhere and took pictures of everything. All these photos were developed and reviewed before being published. If you were in one of these shots you could request a copy of it, so I do have several pictures of me with the President because of those photos. The catch twenty-two about photos however, is we were told to stay out of photos, don't be in the background, don't be in official photo. This was part of our operational security. We were supposed to do our mission and not be seen.

One of the several pictures of me with the President

There were certain times that getting a photo with the President was very acceptable. When you were at the end of your tour of duty at The White House the word would get around that this was your last trip, or close to your last trip on the road with the President. When the Staff and The White House photographer heard this. They would make sure that the President stopped and shook your hand and an official photograph was made. Then, later after the photos were released by the reviewers you would get a nice note from the photo office that there was a package for you to picked up. In it would be multiple copies of the picture they took of you and the President. They treated you just like one of the Presidents VIP or celebrities. It was always nice to get some pat on the back for all the hard work getting a photo packet and a photo with the President was a very nice way to pat the hardworking individuals at The White House.

Military members that worked at The White House as I stated in Chapter 3 almost always had to wear civilian cloths when working around the President and therefore any picture that you may take with the president was in civilian clothes, mostly a coat and tie. There was one exception to this rule, when you were getting ready to leave your duty at The White House your name would be put on the list to have an official picture with the President. Once a month, on the President's schedule was set aside for official military pictures in the Oval Office. This was the one chance you got to have a picture with the President in your official military duty uniform. This was one of the biggest benefits for working so closely with the President and his staff.

However, President Clinton, often cancelled the military photo sessions. I put my name on the list four months out to get a picture with the President. I was on the list at The White House in my full duty uniform for my photo opportunity with the President. President Clinton four months in a row cancelled this time on his calendar at the last minute and I never did get a picture in the Oval Office with President Clinton. This just went along with his continuing of not carrying about the military support that he received. He didn't understand or didn't care how much we worked for him and did for the Office of the Presidency and the very little we ask for in return. Between not coming down and taking pictures with the military families at Christmas time, to not setting aside time to do Oval office pictures. The military was treated like dirt, not respected, and he did not seem to care about us at all. I do not have one picture of me in uniform with the President after supporting the President for over four years.

MY MOM MEETS THE PRESIDENT

When I found out that I was doing the trip to West Palm Beach for the Presidents, I told my mom that I had a surprise for her and for her to come visit me in West Palm Beach during the President's visit. My surprise for her was I got her into the handshake line at the bottom of the steps of Air Force One. If you know the right people and they owe you some favors you can get anyone into a handshake line and get their picture taken with the President.

I had been working with The White House staff for over four years, they knew who I was and what I did. I was always willing to help people out when they had communications or technology issues. I stayed within my military guidelines but I was able to help folks within those guidelines. I told The White House Staff that I was a short timer and that I was leaving The White House soon. I told them that this was a hometown trip for me, and that my Mom was coming to visit me. I asked if I could get my

Mom on the handshake line and of course they said yes. I turned in my Mom's information to the Secret Service so she could get a background check and so I could get her inside the security circle around the President.

My Mom thought she was just coming to stand behind the rope line to see Air Force One land, but when she arrived I came and got her. I brought her out to the tarmac and put her in line with some of the other VIPs that were there, like the Governor of Florida, or the Mayer of West Palm Beach. This was a big thrill for me to get my Mom out in the VIP line. I was happy with that. I left my Mom in line to get her handshake with the President and I went back to stand next to the Motorcade with the other workers. I was so happy I could get my Mom up there, it made me smile.

Air Force One landed and pulled into its space and the mobile stairs were put in place and the President would come out and stop and wave at the media and the people behind the security robe/barricade line. As the President came out of Air Force Once and was waving to the crowd, the White House Staff Lead came up to me and said he had a surprise for me. He took me up to the handshake line and stood me next to my Mom. He turned to me and he thanked me for all that I had done for him and his team. We had worked together for years and he was an ok guy. The President came down the line with an aide next to him telling him the names of the people he was hand shaking. The Official Photographer walks down the line with the President and takes pictures of the President shaking hands and those official photos are provided to the individuals as a memento of this event.

Introducing my mom to President Clinton

The President got to me and the White House Staff Lead was standing with me, told the President that I was finishing up my time with The White House and that my Mom was here with me. The President stopped, thanked me for my service and talked to Mom. He told my Mom how much he enjoyed having me at The White House and that he really valued my support. He brought the official photographer over and took several pictures of use.

The Official Photo

297

The President had that skill to make you feel like you are the most important person in the room and he had done that when talking to my mom. He really made me sound fantastic to my Mom. I don't think my Mom could have been prouder of me then at that moment. The President went on to his limo "The Beast" and the motorcade left. Then I told my Mom that I had one more surprise for her, a VIP tour of Air Force One!

TOUR OF AIR FORCE ONE

The longer you're at The White House the more things you learn and the more people you meet. I had learned that if you talked to the right person at the right stops for Air Force One you could get a VIP tour of the plane. This stop was a quick down and back for the President. The plane did not need to be refueled, it did not need to be serviced, it was just sitting at the airport waiting for the President to come back from his event in West Palm Beach. I made arrangements to get my Mom and my name on the VIP tour list. I had been on Air Force One before but not as a tourist. It was kind of neat to play the tourist with no military duty requirements.

After the motorcade left the airport, those people on the list got in line at the airplane to go through the magnetometer again. Even if you got mag'ed to get into the crowd area you had to get mag'ed again to get on the plane. You had to give up your camera, cellphone, backpack, etc. You couldn't take anything on with you. They set up a table to go through purses and had bags for you to put your things into and had the magnetometers at the bottom of the stairs. We watched them set all this up and then got in line like the other VIPs. After we went through security, handled by the

Air Force members of the Air Force One crew, we were escorted up to the top of the air stairs to the door that the president comes out of. At the top we either had to take off our shoes and leave them there or put on shoe booties/covers. This is to protect the carpet on Air Force One so it stays in outstanding shape. We got to poke our heads into the front cabin that is the Presidential Suite. We got to look into the President's Office that is in the front of the plane and then toured the rest of the plane, the galley, the medical bay, the seating areas for both the press in the back of the plane and The White House staff in the middle of the plane. Then finally we were taken to the Conference room area in the front middle of the plane. We all sat down in the conference room and watched a short move on the TV screens about Air Force one, we were served drinks, and given a little VIP packet of stuff from the plane. I still have some of the items in the VIP packet, that brings nice memories of my time on board this fantastic plane.

Since I have left the job at The White House a very nice video about Air Force One has been put out by the Public Broadcasting System (PBS) and another one by the History Channel. This video shows a tour of Air Force One and shows those things that I talked about.

CHAPTER 14
Life After The White House

After you do the most fascinating job in the world and you are at the top of the mountain of success, then what? After I left The White House, how would I measure my worth and my career success? These were questions others would ask me, my response was that they were asking the wrong question. I had just closed one chapter of my life and was opening new chapters with different challenges leading in different directions. I did not and do not measure myself in work standards.

FAMILY CHALLENGES

After working so hard at The White House, throwing everything I had into my job day after day for four and a half years it had taken a toll on my personal life. My kids were troopers they were young and were flexible through the whole four plus years. They just saw dad working like I always did. They had gotten tired of The White House and maybe didn't really understand what their dad did, supporting the government and the President. They got to the point where they would say "Do we have to go back to The White House again?", "Do we have to meet the President again?" It was nothing really special to them, it was just dad's job that he couldn't talk much about.

My wife and I, on the other hand had changed over the years and we had drifted apart. She kept saying it was the Army life, it was the long hours, the moves, the travel, the time away from her family, and other things. She had been a trooper for over four years taking care of the kids and being a supportive Army wife. I asked my wife where she wanted to go, what she wanted to do. She had followed me around for over twenty years, move after move in the military. Now it was her chance to pick were she wanted to live. She wanted to go back to Peachtree City, Georgia, the city we had moved away from just four and a half years before. She wanted to go back south, away from the snow and back closer to her family in Florida.

When we got ready to leave The White House, it is one of those magical times in your military career where you can tell the big Army at the Pentagon where you wanted to go and what job you wanted. After all, when you get a letter from the President saying that LTC Gelhardt wanted to go back to the Atlanta, Georgia area and to find him a job at that location what could the Pentagon do – say no to the President, of course not.

We got to move back to the Atlanta area, to Peachtree City. We found an empty lot and built a house from scratch. We put the kids back into the Peachtree City school system, where they already had friends from when we lived here before. My wife had friends already and I thought life would just go on and even get better.

I had a good military job as the Chief Information Officer for First U.S. Army at Fort Gillem, in Forest Park outside of Atlanta. We had been back in Peachtree City for about eighteen months and had just moved into the house we had built. I came out on the promotion list to Colonel and I got a call from the Pentagon; they asked me to move back to D.C. to run the National Military Command Center at the Pentagon which was a one star, Brigadier General position. I was on an upward mobile track and there was more for me to do in the military to climb the mountain even higher and maybe even become a general officer, after all that is what the Army was telling me. Didn't every officer in the military dream of being a General Officer?

But I knew family had to come first in this chapter of my life. I had made my choice and pick my family over my career. I wanted to do whatever it would take to save my marriage and I thought getting out of the Army and take the Army out of the equation would be the right thing to do. By now I had been in active Army service for well over the twenty years needed to retire. I could allow my kids to graduate from the same high school, to let them build roots in a community and for me and my wife to work on our relationship.

I retired from the service. However, even though I retired from the service and took a civilian job working as the Chief Information Officer for a charter airline in Peachtree City, I was not able to save my marriage. My wife and I had changed to much. I wanted to go to counseling to see if that would fix our issue, but that did not happen. I don't know if it was my work at The White House that put too big of a gap between her and I, or the twenty-two years in the Army as an Army wife, or maybe it was me? The divorce was devastating to me. I wish my ex-wife well and hope she finds what she is looking for in life.

TELLING STORIES

I have worked hard and am a good person. I give back to my community, I volunteer, and I try and live a good life and treat others the same way I would like to be treated. Life had been good to me up until my divorce, which was the lowest point in my life and when I hit rock bottom.

But life has a way of balancing out a sole. Life has lead me to a second marriage, with a wonderful woman, Karen, my soul mate. We have been together for twelve years now. She was not with me during my military years so she has asked me questions and has listened to me tell my military stories over and over again. She has encouraged me to tell others my stories and has helped me improve my skills in writing and storytelling.

Because of Karen I joined a local Toastmaster Club in Peachtree City, part of Toastmasters International. I have greatly improved my speech giving and storytelling skills to the point that I have been awarded the Distinguished Toastmaster (DTM) certification. She has encouraged me to not only tell my stories but to put them down on paper. I didn't really think I had enough stories that anyone would want to listen to until last November. Karen's son, Matt who was a Captain in the U.S. Army and his lovely new wife Sara were moving from Fort Benning, in Columbus Georgia to Fort Lewis-McCord, in Washington State. This was going to be a four-day, twelve hour a day driving across the nation. Matt and Sara were going to do this move all on their own, with a U-Haul pulling a car and a car pulling a jeep. I volunteered to help Matt and Sara and drove the U-Haul across country on this adventure. Sara joined me in the U-Haul and we started driving across our nation. Sara and I didn't really know each other well so we both started talking and telling stories. Over the next four days we both told stories for almost twelve hours straight each of four days. At the end of that trip I knew I had enough to put down into a book. I only wish I would have recorded all those stories I told her during that trip but I didn't.

THE DECISION TO WRITING A BOOK

Telling stories and giving speeches, which I love to do, and is easy for me is one thing. Deciding to write a book is much different then telling short stories. Stories are short vignettes that tell one story or moral, that can make you laugh or cry. Writing a book with a story line that people want to read from cover to cover is much different. I struggled with this whole idea of writing a book for others to read vs just writing a book for my family and friends. I started doing research on what it takes to write and publish a book and decided to go for it.

During a discussion with my son, David one-day a while back I remember him telling me that he was glad that I had given him a White House tie-tack with the President's Seal and President Clinton's signature on it as a gift. It allowed him to show his friends and tell his own stories about his dad's time at The White House. My kids (David and Kris) were young children when I worked at The White House and may not remember all the same things I do the same way. I tell them that they said "Do we really have to go to The White House again?", they don't remember that. Kris told me one time just recently that she wished she could remember more about that time in our family life, living in Germany, moving around, and our time in D.C. She wished she would have paid some more attention during that part of our lives.

Thanks to David and Kris, I wanted to pass something on to them that they could keep and show others, after all its not every Dad that can say they worked for a President. I wanted my kids, my family, and my friends to have some of these stories, so hence the book.

I hope anyone that reads this enjoys the vignettes, the stories, like the one about "Nametags are important" or "Phone keeps ringing" etc. I hope they put a smile on your face and provide you with some insight to the wonderful military members that work so hard to keep you safe and your government running.

Thank you for reading my book!

If you like this book I now plan on writing a couple of other books about my military career, leadership, and about volunteerism and giving back – look for them coming soon.

30644995R00176

Made in the USA
Columbia, SC
29 October 2018